Food & Wine Guru's Words of Wine Translator

English to French, German, Italian, Spanish, and Back Again

Copyright 2017 Food & Wine Guru
ISBN 978-1-947479-04-3

Food & Wine Guru
B&C Publishing
Box 10206
Aspen, CO 81612

English - French

English	French
Acescence	Acescence
Acetaldehyde	Acétaldéhyde
Acetic	Acétique
Acetone	Acétone
Acid	Acide
Acidic	Acide
Acidity	Acidité
Acquired Alcohol	Alcool Acquis
Acrid	Âcre
Aerobic	Aérobie
Aftertaste	Arrière-Goût
Aftertaste	Arrière-Goût
Aftertaste	Arrière-Goût
Aftertaste	En Fin De Bouche
Age	Vieillir
Age (To)	Élever
Aged	Vieillissement/Élevage
Aged	Vieillissement
Aged Wine	Vin De Garde

English	French
Aging	Vieillissement
Aging	Élevage
Agressive	Agressif
Albumin/Egg White	Albumine
Alcohol	Alcool
Alcoholic	Alcooleux
Alcoholic Fermentation	Fermentation Alcoolique
Alcoholization	Alcoolisation
Alcoholmeter	Alcoomètre
Aldehyde	Aldéhyde
Amber	Ambre
Amberish	Ambré
Angular	Arête
Animal	Animal
Anthocyan	Anthocyane
Anthocyanin	Anthocyanine
Appellation System (Ava)	Appellation D'origine Contrôlée
Aroma	Arôme

English	French
Aromatic	Aromatique
Aromatic Expression	Expression Aromatique
Astringency	Astringence
Astringent	Astringent
Attack	Attaque
Attack	Attaque
Austere	Austère
Bakery	Pâtisserie
Balance	Équilibre
Balance	Étoffé
Balanced	Équilibré
Balling Degree	Degré Balling
Balsamic	Balsamique
Barrel	Barrique
Base Wine	Vin De Base
Bell Pepper	Poivron
Berry	Grain
Berry	Baie
Beta-Glucosidase	Beta-Glucosidase

English	French
Big/Generous Wine	Vin Généreux
Bitter	Amer
Bitter	Acerbe
Bitterness	Amer/Amertume
Bivarietal	Deux Cépages
Black Currant	Cassis
Blanc De Blancs	Blanc De Blancs
Bland	Mou
Blend	Assemblage
Blend	Coupage/Mélange
Bloom	Pruine
Blue/Iron Casse	Casse Ferrique
Botrytis Cinerea (Noble Rot)	Pourriture Noble
Botrytized	Botrytisé
Bottle	Embouteiller/Mettre En Bouteilles
Bottle-Induced Maceration	Macération Induite En Bouteille
Bottle-Stink	Bouteille (Puanteur De)

English	French
Bottled/Bottling	Mise En Bouteilles
Bottling Machine	Machine À Embouteiller
Bouquet (Tertiary Aroma)	Bouquet
Break The Cap/Punch Down	Casser Le Chapeau
Breathing	Respiration
Brilliance	Brillance
Brilliant	Brillant
Brix Degree	Degré Brix
Broken	Cassé
Brut	Brut
Bucket	Godets
Bulk Wine	Vin En Vrac
Burnt	Brûlé
Butter	Beurre
Buttery	Beurré
Cap	Chapeau
Carafe	Bonbonne

English	French
Caramelized	Caramélisé
Carbon Dioxide	Anhydride Carbonique
Carbonated	Gazéifié
Carbonic Gas	Gaz Carbonique
Carbonic Maceration	Macération Carbonique
Carmine	Carmin
Cask	Loger
Cask	Cuve
Cask	Fût
Cask	Bordelaise
Casse	Casse
Cassis	Cassis
Caustic (Overly Sharp)	Mordant
Cedar	Cèdre
Cellar	Cave
Centrifuge	Centrifuger
Champagne Method	Méthode Champenoise
Chaptalization	Chaptalisation

English	French
Character	Caractère
Charmat Method	Méthode Charmat
Cherry (Sour)	Griotte
Cherry (Sweet)	Cerise
Cherry Red (Color)	Rouge Cerise
Chilled	Frappé
Citrus	Citrique
Claret	Clairet
Clarify	Débourrer
Clarifying	Débourrement
Clarity	Clarté
Clear	Propre
Closed	Renfermé/Fermé
Clove	Clou De Girofle
Cloying	Écœurant
Cluster	Grappe
Cold Maceration	Macération À Froid
Colorimeter	Colorimètre
Colouring Material	Matière Colorante

English	French
Compact	Compact
Complex	Complexe
Concentrated Must	Moût Concentré
Cool	Frapper
Cooled	Frappé
Cooper	Tonnelier
Cooper	Fabriquer Des Fûts/ Tonellerie
Cooperage	Tonnellerie
Cordon	Cordon
Cork	Bouchon
Cork Taint (Tca)	Goût De Bouchon
Cream Of Tartar	Crème De Tartre
Crisp	Vivace
Crush/Grind	Fouler
Crusher	Fouloir
Crusher/Grinder	Fouloir
Crushing/Grinding	Foulage
Crust/Sediment	Dépôt En Croûte

English	French
Dates (Fruit)	Dates
Decant	Décanter
Decanter	Carafe
Decanting	Décanté
Decanting Basket/ Cradle	Panier-Verseur
Decanting Cradle/ Basket	Panier-Verseur
Decasked	Décuvé
Decasking	Décuvage
Decrepit	Éventé
Defective	Défectueux
Delicate	Délicat
Demijohn	Dame-Jeanne
Demisec	Demi-Sec
Deposit	Dépôt
Dessert/Sweet Wine	Vin Doux
Destem	Égrapper
Destemmer	Érafloir
Destemmer	Égrappoir

English	French
Destemming	Égrappé
Destemming	Égrappage/Éraflage
Developed	Épanoui
Developed	Évolué
Development Notes	Notes D'évolution
Dill	Aneth
Disgorge	Dégorger
Disgorgement	Dégorgeage
Distinctive	Distinctif
Distinguished	Distingué
Distributor	Débitant
Done	Fait
Dosage	Liqueur D'expédition
Drain	Égoutter
Drainage	Drainage
Drainers	Égouttoir
Dregs/Lies	Lie
Dried Fruits	Fruits Secs
Dry	Sec/Sèche

English	French
Earthy	Terreux
Edge (On The)	Liséré
Effervescence	Effervescence
Effervescent	Effervescent
Egg White/Albumin	Albumine
Egg Whites	Blanc D'œuf
Elegant	Élégant
Enophile	Œnophile
Enzyme	Enzyme
Estate	Domaine/Propriété
Ester	Ester
Ethanol	Éthanol
Ethereal	Éthéré
Ethyl Acetate	Acétate D'éthyle
Extract	Extrait
Fat	Gras
Feel	Touche
Ferment	Fermenter
Fermentation	Fermentation

English	French
Fermentation Trap	Cuve De Fermentation
Filter	Filtrer
Filtering	Filtration
Filtering	Filtrage
Fine	Fin
Fine (To Clarify)	Clarifier
Fining	Clarification
Finish	Fini
Finish (To)	Finir
Fire Engine Red	Rouge Feu
Firm	Ferme
First Press Wine	Vin De Goutte
Flat	Faible
Flavor	Saveur
Flavorful	Savoureux
Fleeting	Fugace
Fleshy	Corpulent
Flexible	Flexible/Souple
Flint	Graves

English	French
Flinty	Goût De Pierre À Fusil
Float	Flotter
Floral	Floral
Flute	Flûte
Foam	Mousse
Fortified	Fortifié
Fortified	Fortifié
Fortified	Aviné
Fortified Wine	Vin Alcoolisé
Fortified Wine	Vin Fortifié
Fortified Wine	Vin De Liqueur
Free-Run Juice	Jus D'égouttage/Jus De Goutte
Fresh	Frais/Fraîche
Fruity	Fruité
Fruity	Fruité
Full	Dense
Full-Bodied	Ample
Garlicy	Odeur D'ail

English	French
Garnet-Red	Grenat
Generic	Générique
Generous	Généreux
Generous/Big Wine	Vin Généreux
Geranium	Géranium
Ginger	Gingembre
Glucan	Glucane
Glycerin	Glycérine
Glycerol	Glycérol
Glycosidade	Glycosidase
Golden	Doré
Grape	Raisin
Grape Seed	Pépin
Grapefruit	Pamplemousse
Grapevine	Vigne
Grassy/Herbacious	Herbacé
Green	Vert
Green Apples	Pomme Verte
Green Wine	Verju

English	French
Greenness/ Herbaceous	Verdeur
Grind/Crush	Fouler
Grinder/Crusher	Fouloir
Grinding/Crushing	Foulage
Grower	Producteur
Gum Arabic	Gomme Arabique
Hard	Dur
Harsh	Dur
Harvest (The)	Vendange
Harvest (To)	Récolte
Heady	Impétueux
Heavy	Lourd
Herbaceous/ Greenness	Verdeur
Herbacious/Grassy	Herbacé
Highlights	Scintillement
Highlights	Teintes
Hint	Note
Hogshead	Baril

English	French
Hollow	Trou
Hopper	Conquet
Horizontal Shakers	Machine À Vendanger
Hose	Tuyau
Hot (Alcohol)	Pointe
Hue	Tonalité
Hue	Teinte
Hue	Tonalité
Hues	Nuances
Icon Wine	Vin Emblématique
Impoverished	Pauvre
Incense	Encens
Incisive	Incisif
Inky	Encre De Chine
Insipid	Insipide
Intense	Intense
Intensity	Intensité
Iron/Blue Casse	Casse Ferrique
Jasmin	Jasmin

English	French
Juice	Jus
Label	Étiquette
Lactic Acid	Acide Lactique
Lanolin	Lanoline
Late	Tardif
Late Harvest	Vendange Tardive
Leather	Cuir
Lee	Lie (De Vin)
Lees	Lie
Legs/Tears	Jambe/Larme
Light	Léger
Limpidity	Limpidité
Lingering	Longue/Prolongé
Liqueur De Tirage (From French)	Liqueur De Tirage
Liquor	Liqueur
Long	Long
Maceration	Macération
Maderized	Boisé

English	French
Maderized (Oxidized Aroma)	Nez Oxydé
Mahogany	Acajou
Main Fermentation	Fermentation Principale
Malic	Malique
Malic Acid	Acide Malique
Malolactic Casse	Casse Malolactique
Malolactic Fermentation	Fermentation Malolactique
Maturation	Maturation
Mature	Mûr
Mature	Mûrir
Meager (Lacking Flavor)	Petit Vin/Maigre
Meaty	Charnu
Meniscus	Ménisque
Menthol	Menthol
Mentholated	Mentholé
Middle Palate	Milieu De Bouche
Mineral	Minéral

English	French
Minerality/Mineral Aromas	Arômes Minéraux
Mineraly	Notes Minérales
Mistelle	Mistelle
Mouthfeel	Saveur En Bouche
Mucilage	Muselage
Muscat	Muscat
Muscat Like	Muscaté
Muselet/Wire Cage (For Champagne Corks)	Muselet
Must	Moût
Naturally Sweet	Douceur Naturelle
Neck	Goulot/Cou
Neck	Goulot/Cou
Neutral	Neutre
New	Nouveau
New (Nouveau) Wine	Vin De L'année
Noble Rot (Botrytis Cinerea)	Pourriture Noble
Nose	Nez

English	French
Nuances	Nuances
Nutmeg	Noix De Muscade
Oak	Chêne
Oak Chips	Copeaux De Bois
Oak Hints	Notes De Bois
Oily	Huileux
Opalescent	Opalescent
Opaque	Opaque
Open	Ouvert
Orange Peel	Zeste D'orange
Ordinary Wine	Vin Ordinaire
Organoleptic	Organoleptique
Overwhelming/ Penetrating (Aroma Or Taste)	Pénétrant
Oxidation	Oxydation
Oxidative Aging	Élevage Oxydatif
Oxidized	Oxydé
Oxidized Nose/ Maderized	Nez Oxydé

English	French
Pair	Marier
Pairing	Mariage
Palate	Saveur/Goût
Pale	Pâle
Paste Like	Pâteux
Pasteurization	Pasteurisation
Pasteurize	Pasteuriser
Penetrating/ Overwhelming (Aroma Or Taste)	Pénétrant
Perfumed	Parfumé
Persistence	Persistance
Phenol	Phénol
Phenolic	Phénolique
Plum	Prune
Polish (Sandblast)	Sabler
Polyphenol	Polyphénol
Pomace	Marc
Potassium Bitartrate	Bitartrate De Potassium

English	French
Potential Alcohol	Alcool En Puissance/ Alcool Potentiel
Potentiality	Potentialité
Precipitant/Sediment	Déposer/Sédimenter
Precipitate	Précipiter
Precipitation	Précipitation
Precipitation/ Sedimentation	Dépôt/Sédimentation
Premium	Premium
Premium Wine	Gamme
Press (To)	Presser
Press Wine	Vin De Presse
Pressing	Pressurage
Pressings	Foulé
Prickly (Nose)	Aigu
Producer	Producteur
Productive	Productif
Productivity	Productivité
Pulp	Pulpe
Pump Over	Remonter

English	French
Pumping	Pompage
Punch Down/Break The Cap	Casser Le Chapeau
Purity	Pureté
Purple	Pourpre
Rack	Soutirer
Racking	Tirage/Soutirage
Raisin Wine	Vin De Paille
Raisining	Passerillage
Raspberry	Framboise
Recall	Rappeler
Rectified Alcohol	Alcool Rectifié
Red	Rouge
Red (For Wine)	Rouge
Red Fruit	Fruits Rouges
Reduction	Réduction
Reductive Aromas	Arômes De Réduction
Refractometer	Réfractomètre
Refractometry	Réfractométrie

English	French
Refresh	Rafraîchir
Reserve	Réserve
Residual Sugar	Sucre Résiduel
Resin	Résine
Rest	Reposer
Rest	Repos
Riddling	Remontage
Ripe Skin	Pellicule Mûre
Robust	Corpulent
Robust	Robuste
Roller	Rouleau
Rolling	Bâtonnage
Rolling	Enfoncement Du Chapeau
Room Temperature	Température Ambiante
Rosé	Rosé
Rotten Egg	Œufs Pourris
Rough	Dur
Round	Rond

English	French
Roundness	Rondeur
Rubbery	Gommeux
Ruby	Rubis
Scales	Échelle
Secondary Fermentation	Seconde Fermentation
Sediment	Sédiment/Dépôt
Sediment/Crust	Dépôt En Croûte
Sediment/Precipitant	Déposer/Sédimenter
Sedimentation/ Precipitation	Dépôt/Sédimentation
Seed	Pépin
Serious	Sérieux
Settle	Laisser Reposer
Settling (Sediment)	Décantation
Shaking Table	Pupitre
Sherrified/Maderized	Saveur Du Sherry
Sherrified/Maderized	Saveur De Madère
Shiny	Satiné

English	French
Short Time In Barrel	Léger Passage En Bois/En Barrique
Shredder	Broyeur
Silky	Soyeux
Singed	Roussi
Skin	Pellicule
Slightly Sparkling Wine	Vin Pétillant
Sluggish Fermentation	Fermentation Lente
Smelling Phase	Olfactif
Smoky	Fumé
Soft	Suave
Softness	Douceur
Sound (Not Bad)	Franc
Sparkling	Mousseux
Sparkling Wine	Vin Mousseux
Spicy	Épicé
Spicy Hot	Piquant
Stabilisation	Stabilisation
Stabilise	Stabiliser

English	French
Stable	Stable
Stained	Taché
Stalk	Rafle
Stalk	Rafle
Stave	Douelle
Stave/Slat	Baguette
Still Wine	Vin Tranquille
Stirring Up	Remuage/Brassage
Stopper	Bouchon
Storage	Stockage
Storage	Emmagasinage
Store	Emmagasiner
Straw (Color)	Paillé
Straw Wine	Vin De Paille
Strawberry	Fraise
Strong	Fort
Structure	Structure
Stuck Fermentation	Fermentation Arrêtée/Suspendue

English	French
Substantial	Mœlleux/Qui A De La Substance
Subtle	Subtil
Succinic Acid	Acide Succinique
Sulfate	Sulfate
Sulfited	Sulfitage
Sulfurous	Soufré (Vin)
Sulphur	Soufre
Sulphur (To)	Méchage/Soufré
Sumptuous	Somptueux
Suspended Solids	Particules Solides En Suspension
Sweet	Abocado
Sweet	Doux
Sweet/Dessert Wine	Vin Doux
Sweetness	Douceur
Syrup	Sirop
Syrupy	Liquoreux
Table Grape	Raisin De Table
Table Wine	Vin De Table

English	French
Tank	Cuve
Tank	Cuve
Tannic	Tanique
Tannin	Tanin
Tap (On A Barrel)	Robinet
Tap (To Tap Barrel)	Perce
Tartaric Acid	Acide Tartrique
Tartrate	Tartrate
Taste	Déguster
Taste (To)	Déguster
Taster	Dégustateur
Tasting (Event)	Dégustation
Tasting (To Be)	Dégustation
Tasting Phase	Gustatif
Tenacity	Ténacité
Tenderness	Tendre
Terpene	Terpène
Terpenic	Terpénique
Terroir	Terroir

English	French
Tertiary Aroma (Bouquet)	Arôme Tertiaire
Texture	Texture
Thin (Lacking Acid)	Décharné/Maigre
Toasted	Grillé
Tobacco	Cigare/Tabac
Total Acidity	Acidité Totale
Total Alcohol	Alcool Total
Traditional Method	Méthode Traditionnelle
Transport	Transport
Transport (To)	Transporter
Tread (To Press By Foot)	Fouler
Tropical Fruits	Fruits Tropicaux
Truffle	Truffe
Turbid	Trouble
Turbidity	Turbidité
Unbalanced	Déséquilibré
Unctuous (Overly Sweet)	Onctueux

English	French
Unripe Berry	Manne
Vanilla	Vanille
Vanilla	Vanillé
Varietal	Vin De Cépage
Varietal Wine	Vin De Cépage
Variety Of Vine/Cultivar	Cep
Cultivar/Variety Of Vine	Cep
Variety Of Grape/ Cultivar	Cépage
Cultivar/Variety Of Grape	Cépage
Varnish	Vernis
Vat	Cuve
Velvety	Velouté
Vigorous	Vigoureux
Vigorous Fermentation	Fermentation Tumultueuse
Vineyard	Vignoble
Vinification/Wine-Making	Vinification
Vinous	Vinosité

English	French
Vintage (Year)	Millésime
Violet (Color)	Violacé
Viscosity	Viscosité
Viscous	Visqueux
Visual Phase	Visuel
Viticulture	Viticulture
Volatile Acidity	Acidité Volatile
Voluptuous	Voluptueux
Walnut	Noix
Warm	Chaud
Watery	Mouillée
Wet Wool	Laine Mouillée
White	Blanc
White Casse	Casse Blanche
Wine	Vin
Wine Alcohol	Alcool De Prestations Viniques
Wine In Carafe	Vin En Carafe/En Pichet
Wine Pipe	Tube

English	French
Wine Press	Pressoir
Wine Press	Pressoir
Wine Steward	Sommelier
Wine Tube/Thief	Dégustateur
Winemaker/Enologist	Œnologue
Enologist/Winemaker	Œnologue
Winemaking And Grape Growing	Vitiviniculture
Winemaking/Enology	Œnologie
Enology/Winemaking	Œnologie
Winery	Cave
Wineskin/Bota Bag	Outre
Wire Cage/Muselet (For Champagne Corks)	Muselet
Yeast	Levure
Yellowish Red/Bricky	Rouge Jaunâtre
Bricky/Yellowish Red	Rouge Jaunâtre
Yield	Rendement
Young	Jeune

English	French
Youth	Jeunesse
Zymurgy	Zimuría

English - German

English	German
Acescence	Essigstich
Acetaldehyde	Acetaldehyd
Acetic	Stichig
Acetone	Keton
Acid	Säure
Acidic	Säuerlich
Acidity	Säuregehalt
Acquired Alcohol	Tatsächlich Entwickelter Alkohol
Acrid	Leicht Säuerlich
Aerobic	Aerob
Aftertaste	Nachgeschmack
Aftertaste	Nachgescmack
Aftertaste	Nachwirkend
Aftertaste	Nachgeschmack
Age	Ablagern
Age (To)	Züchten
Aged	Abgelagert
Aged	Abgelagert
Aged Wine	Alter Von Wein
Aging	Alterung

English	German
Aging	Weinpflege
Agressive	Rauh
Albumin/Egg White	Eiweiß
Alcohol	Alkohol
Alcoholic	Alkoholisch
Alcoholic Fermentation	Alkoholische Gärung
Alcoholization	Alkoholzusatz
Alcoholmeter	Alkoholometer
Aldehyde	Aldehyd
Amber	Amber
Amberish	Bernsteinfarben/ Topasfarben/ Bernsteingelb
Angular	Kantig
Animal	Tieraroma
Anthocyan	Blumenblau
Anthocyanin	Anthocyane
Appellation System (Ava)	Herkunftsbezeichnung
Aroma	Aroma
Aromatic	Aromatisch

English	German
Aromatic Expression	Aromatischer Ausdruck
Astringency	Adstringierender Effekt
Astringent	Adstringierend
Attack	Befall
Attack	Beginn
Austere	Ernst
Bakery	Bäckerei
Balance	Ausgeglichenheit
Balance	Harmonie
Balanced	Ausgeglichen
Balling Degree	Balling-Grade
Balsamic	Balsamisch
Barrel	Kleines Fass
Base Wine	Grundwein
Bell Pepper	Paprika
Berry	Beere
Berry	Beere
Beta-Glucosidase	Betha-Glucosidase
Big/Generous Wine	Feiner Tischwein
Bitter	Bitter

English	German
Bitter	Bitterlich
Bitterness	Bitterkeit
Bivarietal	Verschnitten
Black Currant	Schwarze Johannisbeere
Blanc De Blancs	Blanc
Bland	Fad
Blend	Verschnitt
Blend	Verschnitt
Bloom	Reif
Blue/Iron Casse	Blauwerden
Botrytis Cinerea (Noble Rot)	Edelfäule
Botrytized	Schimmelbefall
Bottle	Abfüllen
Bottle-Induced Maceration	Mazerierung In Der Flasche
Bottle-Stink	Flasche
Bottled/Bottling	Flaschenfüllung
Bottling Machine	Abfüllmaschine
Bouquet (Tertiary Aroma)	Bukett

English	German
Break The Cap/Punch Down	Entkorken
Breathing	Lüftung
Brilliance	Glanz
Brilliant	Glänzend
Brix Degree	Brix-Grade
Broken	Getrübt
Brut	Brut
Bucket	Eimerkette
Bulk Wine	Hauptteilwein
Burnt	Brenzlig/Brandiges Aroma
Butter	Butter
Buttery	Butterig
Cap	Kapsel
Carafe	Karaffe
Caramelized	Aroma Nach Karamel
Carbon Dioxide	Kohlensäure
Carbonated	Mit Kohlensäure
Carbonic Gas	Kohlendyoxid/ Kohlensäure

English	German
Carbonic Maceration	Kohlensäurehaltige Mazeration
Carmine	Karminrot
Cask	Einlagern
Cask	Fass
Cask	Fass
Cask	Tonne
Casse	Bruch
Cassis	Schwarze Johannisbeere
Caustic (Overly Sharp)	Bissig
Cedar	Zeder
Cellar	Weinkeller
Centrifuge	Zentrifugieren
Champagne Method	Flaschengärungverfahren
Chaptalization	Chaptalizierung
Character	Charakter
Charmat Method	Abstichmethode
Cherry (Sour)	Sauerkirsche
Cherry (Sweet)	Kirsche
Cherry Red (Color)	Kirschrot

English	German
Chilled	Gekühlt
Citrus	Zitrusfrucht
Claret	Klarettwein
Clarify	Ohne Bodensatz
Clarifying	Austrieb
Clarity	Klarheit
Clear	Sauber
Closed	Unreif
Clove	Gewürznelke
Cloying	Mostigsüß/Pappsüß/ Widerlich Süß
Cluster	Traube
Cold Maceration	Beerenhautmazeration
Colorimeter	Kolorimeter
Colouring Material	Farbstoff
Compact	Compac
Complex	Komplex
Concentrated Must	Mostkonzentrat
Cool	Abkühlen
Cooled	Tiefgekühlt
Cooper	Böttchermeister

English	German
Cooper	Küpfermeister
Cooperage	Fassbestand
Cordon	Schaumkrone
Cork	Kork
Cork Taint (Tca)	Korkgeschmack
Cream Of Tartar	Weinstein
Crisp	Lebhaft
Crush/Grind	Keltern
Crusher	Traubenmühle
Crusher/Grinder	Kelter
Crushing/Grinding	Kelterung
Crust/Sediment	Farbdepot
Dates (Fruit)	Dattel
Decant	Dekantieren
Decanter	Karaffe
Decanting	Dekantiert
Decanting Basket/Cradle	Dekantierkörbchen
Decanting Cradle/Basket	Dekantierkörbchen
Decasked	Entkapselt

English	German
Decasking	Abstechen
Decrepit	Schal
Defective	Fehlerhaft
Delicate	Delikat
Demijohn	Korbflasche
Demisec	Halbtrocken
Deposit	Niederschlag
Dessert/Sweet Wine	Süßwein
Destem	Abbeeren/Entrappen
Destemmer	Abbeermaschine
Destemmer	Traubenabbeermaschine
Destemming	Abbeeren
Destemming	Schneide Den Traubenstiel
Developed	Aufgeblüht
Developed	Entwickelt
Development Notes	Entwicklungshinweise
Dill	Dill
Disgorge	Ausspeien
Disgorgement	Enthefung

English	German
Distinctive	Sich Unterscheiden
Distinguished	Vornehm
Distributor	Verkäufer
Done	Ausgereift
Dosage	Versandlikör
Drain	Entsaften
Drainage	Dränage
Drainers	Abtropfbrett
Dregs/Lies	Bodensatz
Dried Fruits	Nussgeschmack
Dry	Trocken
Earthy	Bodengeschmack
Edge (On The)	Note
Effervescence	Aufbrausen
Effervescent	Spritzig/Prickeln
Egg White/Albumin	Eiweiß
Egg Whites	Eiweiß
Elegant	Elegant
Enophile	Oenophil
Enzyme	Enzym
Estate	Weingut

English	German
Ester	Ester
Ethanol	Äthanol
Ethereal	Ätherisch
Ethyl Acetate	Essigsäureäthylester
Extract	Extrakt
Fat	Fett
Feel	Hauch
Ferment	Gären/Säuern
Fermentation	Gärung
Fermentation Trap	Gärbehälter
Filter	Filtern
Filtering	Filtern
Filtering	Gefiltert
Fine	Fein
Fine (To Clarify)	Schönen/Klären
Fining	Klärung/Schönung
Finish	Ausgebaut
Finish (To)	Ende
Fire Engine Red	Feurig/Feurigrot
Firm	Fest
First Press Wine	Laufen Wein

English	German
Flat	Flach
Flavor	Geschmack
Flavorful	Lecker
Fleeting	Flüchtig
Fleshy	Körperreich
Flexible	Flexibel
Flint	Kiesgrund
Flinty	Feuersteingeschmack
Float	Schwimmen
Floral	Blütenduft
Flute	Sektglas
Foam	Schaum
Fortified	Alkolholzusatz
Fortified	Ausgespritet
Fortified	Verstärkt
Fortified Wine	Gespriteter Wein
Fortified Wine	Gespriteter Wein
Fortified Wine	Likörwein
Free-Run Juice	Entwässerung Saft
Fresh	Frisch
Fruity	Fruchtig

English	German
Fruity	Fruchtig/Obstig
Full	Dicht
Full-Bodied	Füllig
Garlicy	Knoblaucharoma
Garnet-Red	Granatfarben
Generic	Gattungsbezeichnung
Generous	Generös
Generous/Big Wine	Feiner Tischwein
Geranium	Geranie
Ginger	Ingwer
Glucan	Glucan
Glycerin	Glyzerin
Glycerol	Glyzerol
Glycosidade	Glykosidase
Golden	Goldgelb
Grape	Traube
Grape Seed	Kern
Grapefruit	Pampelmuse
Grapevine	Weinstock
Grassy/Herbacious	Grasig/Grasherb
Green	Grün

English	German
Green Apples	Apfelaroma
Green Wine	Verjus
Greenness/ Herbaceous	Grüngeschmack
Grind/Crush	Keltern
Grinder/Crusher	Kelter
Grinding/Crushing	Kelterung
Grower	Erzeuger
Gum Arabic	Gummi Arabicum
Hard	Hart
Harsh	Hart
Harvest (The)	Traubenernte
Harvest (To)	Ernte
Heady	Herzhaft
Heavy	Schwer
Herbaceous/ Greenness	Grüngeschmack
Herbacious/Grassy	Grasig/Grasherb
Highlights	Funke
Highlights	Schillern
Hint	Note

English	German
Hogshead	Fass
Hollow	Leer
Hopper	Trogförmiger Trichter Der Traubenmühle
Horizontal Shakers	Erntemaschine
Hose	Schlauch
Hot (Alcohol)	Eckig/Kantig
Hue	Farbton
Hue	Ton
Hue	Tönung
Hues	Färbung
Icon Wine	Ikonischen Wein
Impoverished	Arm
Incense	Weihrauchgeruch
Incisive	Schneidig
Inky	Tinte
Insipid	Fad
Intense	Vollmundig/ Körperreich
Intensity	Intensität
Iron/Blue Casse	Blauwerden

English	German
Jasmin	Jasmin
Juice	Saft
Label	Etikett
Lactic Acid	Milchsäure
Lanolin	Lanoline
Late	Hochreif
Late Harvest	Spätlese
Leather	Ledergeruch
Lee	Reife
Lees	Trub
Legs/Tears	Träne
Light	Leicht
Limpidity	Klarheit
Lingering	Lang
Liqueur De Tirage (From French)	Likörartig
Liquor	Likör
Long	Nachhaltig
Maceration	Mazerierung
Maderized	Maderisiert

English	German
Maderized (Oxidized Aroma)	Oxidierte Nase
Mahogany	Mahagonibaum
Main Fermentation	Hauptgärung
Malic	Apfelgeschmack
Malic Acid	Apfelsäure
Malolactic Casse	Quebradura Maloláctica
Malolactic Fermentation	Apfel-Milchsäure-Gärung
Maturation	Reifen
Mature	Reif
Mature	Reif/Gereift
Meager (Lacking Flavor)	Überstreckt
Meaty	Fleischig
Meniscus	Meniskus
Menthol	Menthol
Mentholated	Mit Menthol
Middle Palate	Mitte Gaumen
Mineral	Mineralisch
Minerality/Mineral Aromas	Mineralisches Aroma

English	German
Mineraly	Mineralisch
Mistelle	Mistela
Mouthfeel	Organoleptische Empfindung
Mucilage	Muselage
Muscat	Muskateller
Muscat Like	Muskatbukett/ Muskattellerton
Muselet/Wire Cage (For Champagne Corks)	Bügelverschluss
Must	Most
Naturally Sweet	Natursüße
Neck	Flaschenhals
Neck	Flaschenhals
Neutral	Neutral
New	Neuer Wein
New (Nouveau) Wine	Neuer Wein
Noble Rot (Botrytis Cinerea)	Edelfäule
Nose	Nase
Nuances	Nuance
Nutmeg	Muskatnuss

English	German
Oak	Eiche
Oak Chips	Eichen-Chips
Oak Hints	Holzgeschmack
Oily	Ölig
Opalescent	Opalisierend
Opaque	Undurchsichtig
Open	Anämisch
Orange Peel	Orangenschale
Ordinary Wine	Einfach
Organoleptic	Organoleptisch
Overwhelming/ Penetrating (Aroma Or Taste)	Aufsteigend/ Aufdringlich
Oxidation	Oxidierung
Oxidative Aging	Alterungsprozess Oxidation
Oxidized	Versiedet/Oxidiert
Oxidized Nose/ Maderized	Oxidierte Nase
Pair	Eng Verbinden
Pairing	Enge Verbindung
Palate	Gaumen

English	German
Pale	Bleich
Paste Like	Zähflüssig
Pasteurization	Pasteurisieren
Pasteurize	Pasteurisieren
Penetrating/ Overwhelming (Aroma Or Taste)	Aufsteigend/ Aufdringlich
Perfumed	Duftend
Persistence	Nachhaltigkeit
Phenol	Phenol
Phenolic	Phenolisch
Plum	Pflaume
Polish (Sandblast)	Sandeln
Polyphenol	Poliphenole
Pomace	Trester
Potassium Bitartrate	Kaliumbitartrat
Potential Alcohol	Potentiell Vorhandener Alkohol
Potentiality	Kraft
Precipitant/Sediment	Depot Bilden
Precipitate	Ausfällen
Precipitation	Niederschlag

English	German
Precipitation/ Sedimentation	Depot Bildung
Premium	Premiumwein
Premium Wine	Spitzenwein
Press (To)	Pressen
Press Wine	Scheitermost
Pressing	Keltern
Pressings	Auspressen
Prickly (Nose)	Scharf
Producer	Erzeuger
Productive	Ergiebig
Productivity	Produktivität
Pulp	Fruchtfleisch
Pump Over	Umpumpen
Pumping	Abpumpen
Punch Down/Break The Cap	Entkorken
Purity	Reinheit
Purple	Purpurfarben
Rack	Abstechen/Entleeren
Racking	Entleerung

English	German
Raisin Wine	Strohwein
Raisining	Rosinen
Raspberry	Himbeere
Recall	Erinnern
Rectified Alcohol	Rektifizierter Alkohol
Red	Rot
Red (For Wine)	Rotwein
Red Fruit	Beerenaroma
Reduction	Reduktion
Reductive Aromas	Aromen Reduktion
Refractometer	Refraktometer
Refractometry	Refraktometrie
Refresh	Verjüngen
Reserve	Reserve
Residual Sugar	Restzucker
Resin	Geharzt
Rest	Ablagern
Rest	Lager
Riddling	Rütteln
Ripe Skin	Reife Beerenhülse
Robust	Körperreich

English	German
Robust	Robust/Solid
Roller	Rolle
Rolling	Schlagen/Umrühren
Rolling	Unterstoßen
Room Temperature	Raumtemperatur
Rosé	Roséwein
Rotten Egg	Faule Eier
Rough	Hart
Round	Rund
Roundness	Rundung
Rubbery	Gummiartig
Ruby	Rubin
Scales	Staffelung
Secondary Fermentation	Nachgärung
Sediment	Depot
Sediment/Crust	Farbdepot
Sediment/Precipitant	Depot Bilden
Sedimentation/Precipitation	Depot Bildung
Seed	Kern

English	German
Serious	Ernst
Settle	Klären
Settling (Sediment)	Dekantieren
Shaking Table	Mischpult
Sherrified/Maderized	Sherrygeschmack
Sherrified/Maderized	Sherrygeschmack
Shiny	Seidig
Short Time In Barrel	Kurze Zeit In Holz
Shredder	Quetschmaschine
Silky	Seidig
Singed	Fuchsrot
Skin	Beerenhülse
Slightly Sparkling Wine	Perlwein
Sluggish Fermentation	Kaltgärung
Smelling Phase	Olfaktorisch
Smoky	Geräuchert
Soft	Sanft/Geschmeidig
Softness	Milde
Sound (Not Bad)	Reintönig
Sparkling	Schaumwein
Sparkling Wine	Schaumwein

English	German
Spicy	Würzig
Spicy Hot	Scharf
Stabilisation	Ausbau
Stabilise	Ausgleichen
Stable	Stabil
Stained	Verfärbt
Stalk	Rappe
Stalk	Rappen
Stave	Dauben
Stave/Slat	Latte/Leiste
Still Wine	Stillwein
Stirring Up	Umrühren
Stopper	Pfropfen
Storage	Lagern
Storage	Stauung
Store	Stapeln
Straw (Color)	Strohfarben
Straw Wine	Strohwein
Strawberry	Erdbeere
Strong	Stark
Structure	Struktur

English	German
Stuck Fermentation	Gärung Verhaftet
Substantial	Vollmundig/ Körperreich
Subtle	Hochfein
Succinic Acid	Succinsäure
Sulfate	Sulfat
Sulfited	Überschwefelt
Sulfurous	Sulfidisch/ Schwefelhaltig
Sulphur	Schwefel
Sulphur (To)	Schwefeln
Sumptuous	Prachtvoll
Suspended Solids	Schwebstoffe
Sweet	Süß
Sweet	Süß
Sweet/Dessert Wine	Süßwein
Sweetness	Süße
Syrup	Konzentrierter Most
Syrupy	Alkoholreich
Table Grape	Tafeltrauben
Table Wine	Tischwein/Tafelwein

English	German
Tank	Bottich
Tank	Tank
Tannic	Tanninhaltig
Tannin	Gerbstoff
Tap (On A Barrel)	Fasshahn
Tap (To Tap Barrel)	Anstich
Tartaric Acid	Weinsäure
Tartrate	Tartrat
Taste	Kosten/Probieren
Taste (To)	Verkosten
Taster	Weinverkoster
Tasting (Event)	Weinprobe
Tasting (To Be)	Weinprobe/Weinkost
Tasting Phase	Geschmacklich
Tenacity	Nachhalt
Tenderness	Artig
Terpene	Terpene
Terpenic	Terpenisch
Terroir	Boden
Tertiary Aroma (Bouquet)	Tertiäres Aroma

English	German
Texture	Struktur
Thin (Lacking Acid)	Mager/Dünn
Toasted	Geröstet
Tobacco	Tabak
Total Acidity	Gesamtsäure
Total Alcohol	Gesamtalkohol
Traditional Method	Traditionelle Methode
Transport	Transport
Transport (To)	Transportieren
Tread (To Press By Foot)	Lauffläche
Tropical Fruits	Tropenfrüchte
Truffle	Trüffel
Turbid	Trüb
Turbidity	Trübschleier
Unbalanced	Unausgewogen
Unctuous (Overly Sweet)	Geschmeidig
Unripe Berry	Manna
Vanilla	Vanille
Vanilla	Vanillegeschmack/ Vanilleduft

English	German
Varietal	Rebsorte
Varietal Wine	Verschnitt
Variety Of Vine/Cultivar	Rebsorte
Cultivar/Variety Of Vine	Rebsorte
Variety Of Grape/ Cultivar	Rebsorte
Cultivar/Variety Of Grape	Rebsorte
Varnish	Firnis
Vat	Gefäß/Behälte
Velvety	Samtig
Vigorous	Widerstandsfähig
Vigorous Fermentation	Stürmische Gärung
Vineyard	Weinbaugebiet
Vinification/Wine-Making	Weinbereitung
Vinous	Weinig
Vintage (Year)	Jahrgang
Violet (Color)	Violett
Viscosity	Viskozität
Viscous	Zähflüssig
Visual Phase	Visuelle

English	German
Viticulture	Weinbau
Volatile Acidity	Flüchtige
Voluptuous	Vollkommen
Walnut	Walnuss
Warm	Wärmend
Watery	Wässerig
Wet Wool	Feuchte Wolle
White	Weißwein
White Casse	Weisser Bruch
Wine	Wein
Wine Alcohol	Weinalkohol
Wine In Carafe	Einfach
Wine Pipe	Tube
Wine Press	Presse
Wine Press	Presse
Wine Steward	Sommelier
Wine Tube/Thief	Probezieher/ Weinheber
Winemaker/Enologist	Önologe
Enologist/Winemaker	Önologe

English	German
Winemaking And Grape Growing	Weinbau
Winemaking/Enology	Önologie
Enology/Winemaking	Önologie
Winery	Weinkeller
Wineskin/Bota Bag	Lederflasche
Wire Cage/Muselet (For Champagne Corks)	Bügelverschluss
Yeast	Hefe
Yellowish Red/Bricky	Gelbliches Rot
Bricky/Yellowish Red	Gelbliches Rot
Yield	Ertrag
Young	Jung
Youth	Jugend
Zymurgy	Zymurgie

English - Italian

English	Italian
Acescence	Acescenza
Acetaldehyde	Acetaldeide
Acetic	Pungente
Acetone	Acetone
Acid	Acido
Acidic	Ulousacido
Acidity	Acidità
Acquired Alcohol	Alcol Arricchito
Acrid	Acre
Aerobic	Aerobico
Aftertaste	Retrogusto
Aftertaste	Retrogusto
Aftertaste	Retrogusto
Aftertaste	Finale Di Bocca
Age	Invecchiare
Age (To)	Allevare
Aged	Invecchiato
Aged	Invecchiato
Aged Wine	Vino Destinato Al Invecchiamento
Aging	Invecchiamento

English	Italian
Aging	Conservazione
Agressive	Aggressivo
Albumin/Egg White	Albumina
Alcohol	Alcol
Alcoholic	Alcoolato
Alcoholic Fermentation	Fermentazione Alcolica
Alcoholization	Alcoolizzazione
Alcoholmeter	Etilometro
Aldehyde	Aldeide
Amber	Ambra
Amberish	Ambrato
Angular	Angoli
Animal	Animale
Anthocyan	Antociano
Anthocyanin	Antocianina
Appellation System (Ava)	Denominazione Di Origine Controllata
Aroma	Aroma
Aromatic	Aromatico
Aromatic Expression	Espressione Aromatica
Astringency	Astringenza

English	Italian
Astringent	Astringente
Attack	Attacco
Attack	Inizio
Austere	Austero
Bakery	Pasticceria
Balance	Equilibrio
Balance	Armonia
Balanced	Equilibrato
Balling Degree	Grado Di Ballo
Balsamic	Balsamico
Barrel	Barile
Base Wine	Vino Base
Bell Pepper	Peperone Dolce
Berry	Grano
Berry	Acino
Beta-Glucosidase	Beta-Glucoside
Big/Generous Wine	Vino Generoso
Bitter	Amaro
Bitter	Amaro
Bitterness	Amaro
Bivarietal	Bivarietale

English	Italian
Black Currant	Ribes Nero
Blanc De Blancs	Blanc De Blancs
Bland	Molle
Blend	Taglio
Blend	Taglio
Bloom	Pruina
Blue/Iron Casse	Fermentazione Ferrica
Botrytis Cinerea (Noble Rot)	Marciume Nobile
Botrytized	Botritizzata
Bottle	Imbottigliare
Bottle-Induced Maceration	Macerazione Indotta In Bottiglia
Bottle-Stink	Bottiglia (Puzza Di)
Bottled/Bottling	Imbottigliato
Bottling Machine	Imbottigliatrice
Bouquet (Tertiary Aroma)	Insieme Di Profumi
Break The Cap/Punch Down	Rompere Il Cappello Di Fermentazione
Breathing	Respirazione
Brilliance	Brillantezza

English	Italian
Brilliant	Brillante
Brix Degree	Brix
Broken	Rotto
Brut	Brut
Bucket	Secchio
Bulk Wine	Vino Sfuso
Burnt	Bruciato(Sapore/ Gusto)
Butter	Burro
Buttery	Burroso
Cap	Capello
Carafe	Caraffa/Bombola
Caramelized	Caramellato
Carbon Dioxide	Biossido Di Carbonio
Carbonated	Gassoso
Carbonic Gas	Gas Carbonico
Carbonic Maceration	Macerazione Carbonica
Carmine	Rosso Carmine
Cask	Imbottare
Cask	Botte

English	Italian
Cask	Botte
Cask	Barile/Barrica
Casse	Rottura
Cassis	Ribes Nero
Caustic (Overly Sharp)	Mordente
Cedar	Cedro
Cellar	Cantina
Centrifuge	Centrifugare
Champagne Method	Metodo Classico
Chaptalization	Zuccheraggio
Character	Carattere
Charmat Method	Metodo In Autoclave
Cherry (Sour)	Amarena
Cherry (Sweet)	Ciliegia
Cherry Red (Color)	Rosso Ciliegia
Chilled	Ben Freddo
Citrus	Citrico
Claret	Claretto
Clarify	Chiarificare
Clarifying	Chiarifica
Clarity	Chiarezza

English	Italian
Clear	Pulito
Closed	Chiuso
Clove	Chiodi Di Garofano
Cloying	Evole
Cluster	Grappolo
Cold Maceration	Macerazione A Freddo
Colorimeter	Colorimetro
Colouring Material	Materia Colorante
Compact	Compatto
Complex	Complesso
Concentrated Must	Mosto Concentrato
Cool	Raffreddare
Cooled	Raffreddato
Cooper	Bottaio
Cooper	Fabbricare Botti
Cooperage	Fabbrica Di Botte
Cordon	Corona
Cork	Tappo
Cork Taint (Tca)	Sapore Di Sughero
Cream Of Tartar	Cremor Tartaro
Crisp	Vivace

English	Italian
Crush/Grind	Disrapare/Pigliare
Crusher	Pigiatrice
Crusher/Grinder	Pigliatrice
Crushing/Grinding	Pigliatura
Crust/Sediment	Crosta
Dates (Fruit)	Datteri
Decant	Separare
Decanter	Decantatore/Brocca
Decanting	Decantato
Decanting Basket/ Cradle	Cesta
Decanting Cradle/ Basket	Cesta
Decasked	Rimuovere Dalla Botte
Decasking	Svinatura
Decrepit	Svanito
Defective	Difettoso
Delicate	Delicato
Demijohn	Damigiana
Demisec	Demi-Sec
Deposit	Deposito

English	Italian
Dessert/Sweet Wine	Vino Dolce
Destem	Diraspare
Destemmer	Diraspatura
Destemmer	Diraspatura
Destemming	Diraspato
Destemming	Diraspatura
Developed	Sviluppato/Non Sviluppato
Developed	Evoluto
Development Notes	Stati Di Evoluzione
Dill	Aneto
Disgorge	Sgozzare/Aprire
Disgorgement	Sboccatura
Distinctive	Distintivo
Distinguished	Nobile/Austero
Distributor	Distributore
Done	Fatto
Dosage	Liquore Di Spedizione
Drain	Sgrondare
Drainage	Drenato
Drainers	Grondatore

English	Italian
Dregs/Lies	Feccia/Sedimento
Dried Fruits	Frutta Secca
Dry	Secco
Earthy	Terroso
Edge (On The)	Nota
Effervescence	Effervescenza
Effervescent	Effervescente
Egg White/Albumin	Albumina
Egg Whites	Bianco D'uovo/Chiaro D'uovo
Elegant	Elegante
Enophile	Enofilo
Enzyme	Enzima
Estate	Azienda Agricola
Ester	Estere
Ethanol	Etanolo
Ethereal	Etereo
Ethyl Acetate	Acetato Di Etile
Extract	Estratto
Fat	Grasso
Feel	Tocco

English	Italian
Ferment	Fermentare
Fermentation	Fermentazione
Fermentation Trap	Contenitore Di Fermentazione
Filter	Filtrare
Filtering	Filtraggio
Filtering	Filtrato
Fine	Fino
Fine (To Clarify)	Chiarificare
Fining	Chiarifica
Finish	Finito/Pieno
Finish (To)	Terminare
Fire Engine Red	Rosso Fuoco
Firm	Solido
First Press Wine	Vino Di Laccrima
Flat	Debole/Molle
Flavor	Sapore
Flavorful	Saporoso
Fleeting	Fugace
Fleshy	Con Corpo
Flexible	Flessibile

English	Italian
Flint	Ghiaia
Flinty	Pietra Fuocaia/Selce
Float	Galleggiare
Floral	Floreale
Flute	Flute
Foam	Spuma
Fortified	Arricchito
Fortified	Rinforzato
Fortified	Avvinato
Fortified Wine	Alcolizzato Vino
Fortified Wine	Vino Di Aggiunto
Fortified Wine	Vino Liquoroso
Free-Run Juice	Mosto Fiore
Fresh	Fresco
Fruity	Frutato
Fruity	Frutato
Full	Denso
Full-Bodied	Ampio
Garlicy	Oddore Di Aglio
Garnet-Red	Granata
Generic	Generico

English	Italian
Generous	Generoso
Generous/Big Wine	Vino Generoso
Geranium	Geranio
Ginger	Zenzero
Glucan	Gluconato
Glycerin	Glicerina
Glycerol	Glicerolo
Glycosidade	Glucosidasi
Golden	Dorato
Grape	Uva
Grape Seed	Vinacciolo
Grapefruit	Pompelmo
Grapevine	Vite
Grassy/Herbacious	Erbaceo
Green	Verde
Green Apples	Mele Verdi
Green Wine	Duro
Greenness/ Herbaceous	Acerbità
Grind/Crush	Disrapare/Pigliare
Grinder/Crusher	Pigliatrice

English	Italian
Grinding/Crushing	Pigliatura
Grower	Coltivatore
Gum Arabic	Gomma Arabica
Hard	Duro
Harsh	Aspro
Harvest (The)	Vendemmia
Harvest (To)	Raccolto
Heady	Impetuoso
Heavy	Pesante
Herbaceous/ Greenness	Acerbità
Herbacious/Grassy	Erbaceo
Highlights	Vivacità/Brillantezza
Highlights	Fumature
Hint	Nota
Hogshead	Barile
Hollow	Buco
Hopper	Tramoggia Di Scarico
Horizontal Shakers	Macchina A Scuotimento Orizontale
Hose	Tubo Flessibile

English	Italian
Hot (Alcohol)	Prima Sensazione Di Fumo Di Alcool
Hue	Tono
Hue	Inchiostro
Hue	Tonalità
Hues	Sfumature
Icon Wine	Vino Emblematico
Impoverished	Povero
Incense	Incenso
Incisive	Incisivo
Inky	Inchiostro
Insipid	Insipido
Intense	Intenso
Intensity	Intensità
Iron/Blue Casse	Fermentazione Ferrica
Jasmin	Gelsomino
Juice	Succo
Label	Etichetta
Lactic Acid	Acido Lattico
Lanolin	Lanolina
Late	Tardivo

English	Italian
Late Harvest	Vendemmia Tardiva
Leather	Cuoio
Lee	Madre
Lees	Fune
Legs/Tears	Lacrime/Archetti
Light	Leggero
Limpidity	Limpidezza
Lingering	Allungato
Liqueur De Tirage (From French)	Liqueur De Tirage
Liquor	Liquore
Long	Lungo
Maceration	Macerazione
Maderized	Maderizzato/Marsalato
Maderized (Oxidized Aroma)	Sapore Di Ossidato
Mahogany	Mogano
Main Fermentation	Fermentazione Principale
Malic	Malico
Malic Acid	Acido Malico

English	Italian
Malolactic Casse	Fermentazione Interrotta/Malolattica
Malolactic Fermentation	Fermentazione Malolattica
Maturation	Maturazione
Mature	Maturo
Mature	Maturare
Meager (Lacking Flavor)	Annacquato/Aggiunto Di
Meaty	Carnoso
Meniscus	Menisco
Menthol	Mentolo
Mentholated	Mentolo
Middle Palate	Mezzo Palato
Mineral	Minerale
Minerality/Mineral Aromas	Arome Minerali
Mineraly	Tocchi Minerali
Mistelle	Mistella
Mouthfeel	Sensazione Organolettica
Mucilage	Ingabbiettatura
Muscat	Moscato

English	Italian
Muscat Like	Aggiunto Di Moscato
Muselet/Wire Cage (For Champagne Corks)	Gabbietta
Must	Mosto
Naturally Sweet	Dolce Naturale
Neck	Collo
Neck	Nec
Neutral	Neutro
New	Nuovo
New (Nouveau) Wine	Vino Dell'annata
Noble Rot (Botrytis Cinerea)	Marciume Nobile
Nose	Profumo/Odore/Sapore
Nuances	Sfumature
Nutmeg	Noce Moscata
Oak	Rovere/Quercia (Sapore)
Oak Chips	Chips/Segatura
Oak Hints	Tocchi Di Legno
Oily	Oleoso
Opalescent	Opalescente

English	Italian
Opaque	Opaco
Open	Aperto
Orange Peel	Buccia Di Arancia
Ordinary Wine	Vino Senza Qualità
Organoleptic	Organolettico
Overwhelming/ Penetrating (Aroma Or Taste)	Penetrante
Oxidation	Ossidazione
Oxidative Aging	Conservazione In Fase Ossidante
Oxidized	Ossidato
Oxidized Nose/ Maderized	Sapore Di Ossidato
Pair	Mescolare
Pairing	Matrimonio
Palate	Palato
Pale	Pallido
Paste Like	Pastoso
Pasteurization	Pastorizzazione
Pasteurize	Pastorizzare

English	Italian
Penetrating/ Overwhelming (Aroma Or Taste)	Penetrante
Perfumed	Fragrante
Persistence	Persistenza/Tenacita
Phenol	Fenolo
Phenolic	Fenolico
Plum	Pruna/Susina
Polish (Sandblast)	Sabbiare
Polyphenol	Polifenolo
Pomace	Vinaccia
Potassium Bitartrate	Bitartrato Di Potasio
Potential Alcohol	Alcol Potenziale
Potentiality	Potenzialità
Precipitant/Sediment	Precipitare
Precipitate	Precipitare
Precipitation	Precipitazione
Precipitation/ Sedimentation	Sedimentazione/ Precipitazione
Premium	Competitivo
Premium Wine	Gamma
Press (To)	Pressare

English	Italian
Press Wine	Vino Di Pressa/Torchio
Pressing	Pressatura
Pressings	Premitura
Prickly (Nose)	Pungente
Producer	Produttore
Productive	Produttivo
Productivity	Produttività
Pulp	Polpa
Pump Over	Rimontare
Pumping	Pompaggio
Punch Down/Break The Cap	Rompere Il Cappello Di Fermentazione
Purity	Purezza
Purple	Porpora
Rack	Travasare
Racking	Travaso
Raisin Wine	Vino Passito
Raisining	Appasimento
Raspberry	Lampone
Recall	Ricordare
Rectified Alcohol	Alcol Rettificato

English	Italian
Red	Rosso
Red (For Wine)	Colorato/Rosso
Red Fruit	Frutti Di Bosco
Reduction	Riduzione
Reductive Aromas	Sapore Di Ridotto
Refractometer	Rifrattometro
Refractometry	Rifractometria
Refresh	Rinfrescare
Reserve	Riserva
Residual Sugar	Zucchero Residuo
Resin	Resina
Rest	Riposare
Rest	Riposo
Riddling	Rimontaggio
Ripe Skin	Buccia Matura
Robust	Robusto
Robust	Robusto
Roller	Rullo
Rolling	Bastonatura
Rolling	Agitazione
Room Temperature	Temperatura Ambiente

English	Italian
Rosé	Rosato
Rotten Egg	Sapore D'uovo Marchio
Rough	Aspro
Round	Rotondo
Roundness	Rotondità
Rubbery	Gommoso
Ruby	Rubino
Scales	Scala
Secondary Fermentation	Fermentazione Secondaria
Sediment	Precipitato
Sediment/Crust	Crosta
Sediment/Precipitant	Precipitare
Sedimentation/ Precipitation	Sedimentazione/ Precipitazione
Seed	Eme
Serious	Serio
Settle	Invecchiare
Settling (Sediment)	Separazione
Shaking Table	Banco Mobile
Sherrified/Maderized	Marsalato

English	Italian
Sherrified/Maderized	Marsalato
Shiny	Satinato
Short Time In Barrel	Passagio Veloce Per Il Legno
Shredder	Trituratrice
Silky	Setoso
Singed	Con Riflessi Rossi
Skin	Buccia
Slightly Sparkling Wine	Vino Frizzante
Sluggish Fermentation	Fermentazione Lenta
Smelling Phase	Fase Olfattiva
Smoky	Affumicato
Soft	Suave/Morbido
Softness	Morbidezza
Sound (Not Bad)	Franco/Genuino
Sparkling	Spumante
Sparkling Wine	Vino Spumante
Spicy	Speziato
Spicy Hot	Piccante
Stabilisation	Stabilizzazione
Stabilise	Stabilizzare

English	Italian
Stable	Stabile
Stained	Macchiato
Stalk	Raspo
Stalk	Ruvideza
Stave	Doga
Stave/Slat	Bacchetta
Still Wine	Vino Fermo
Stirring Up	Rimosso
Stopper	Tampón
Storage	Immagazzinamento
Storage	Immagazzinaggio
Store	Immagazzinare
Straw (Color)	Paglierino
Straw Wine	Vino Passito
Strawberry	Fragola
Strong	Forte
Structure	Struttura
Stuck Fermentation	Fermentazione Incompleta
Substantial	Sostanzioso
Subtle	Sottile

English	Italian
Succinic Acid	Acido Succinico
Sulfate	Solfato
Sulfited	Solfitato
Sulfurous	Solforoso
Sulphur	Zolfo
Sulphur (To)	Ingzolforato
Sumptuous	Sontuoso
Suspended Solids	Particelle Solide In Sospensione
Sweet	Abbocato
Sweet	Dolce
Sweet/Dessert Wine	Vino Dolce
Sweetness	Dolcezza
Syrup	Sciroppo
Syrupy	Liquoroso
Table Grape	Uva Da Tavola
Table Wine	Vino Da Tavola
Tank	Vasca
Tank	Serbatoio
Tannic	Tannicco
Tannin	Tannino

English	Italian
Tap (On A Barrel)	Rubinetto
Tap (To Tap Barrel)	Ceppo
Tartaric Acid	Acido Tartarico
Tartrate	Tartrato
Taste	Assagiare
Taste (To)	Degustare
Taster	Degustatore
Tasting (Event)	Assaggio
Tasting (To Be)	Degustazione
Tasting Phase	Gustativa
Tenacity	Tenacia
Tenderness	Tenero
Terpene	Terpeno
Terpenic	Terpenico
Terroir	Pezzo Di Terra
Tertiary Aroma (Bouquet)	Aroma Terziario
Texture	Solidità
Thin (Lacking Acid)	Magro
Toasted	Tostato
Tobacco	Tabacco

English	Italian
Total Acidity	Acidità Totale
Total Alcohol	Alcol Totale
Traditional Method	Metodo Tradizionale
Transport	Trasporto
Transport (To)	Trasportare
Tread (To Press By Foot)	Battistrada
Tropical Fruits	Frutti Tropicali
Truffle	Tartufo
Turbid	Torbido
Turbidity	Torbidezza
Unbalanced	Squilibrato
Unctuous (Overly Sweet)	Untuoso
Unripe Berry	Duro
Vanilla	Vaniglia
Vanilla	Sapore Di Vaniglia
Varietal	Varietal
Varietal Wine	Vino Varietale
Variety Of Vine/Cultivar	Ceppo
Cultivar/Variety Of Vine	Ceppo

English	Italian
Variety Of Grape/ Cultivar	Varietà
Cultivar/Variety Of Grape	Varietà
Varnish	Vernice
Vat	Recipiente
Velvety	Complesso/Corposo
Vigorous	Vigoroso
Vigorous Fermentation	Fermentazione Tumultuosa
Vineyard	Vigneto
Vinification/Wine-Making	Vinificazione
Vinous	Vinosità
Vintage (Year)	Annata
Violet (Color)	Violaceo
Viscosity	Viscosita
Viscous	Viscoso
Visual Phase	Visiva
Viticulture	Viticoltura
Volatile Acidity	Acidità Volatile
Voluptuous	Voluttuoso

English	Italian
Walnut	Noce
Warm	Caloroso
Watery	Annacquato
Wet Wool	Lana Bagnata
White	Bianco
White Casse	Nuvola
Wine	Vino
Wine Alcohol	Alcol Vinico
Wine In Carafe	Vino Sfuso/In Caraffa
Wine Pipe	Cannuccia
Wine Press	Tramoggia
Wine Press	Pressa
Wine Steward	Degustatore/Consigliere/Sommelier
Wine Tube/Thief	Degustatore
Winemaker/Enologist	Enologo
Enologist/Winemaker	Enologo
Winemaking And Grape Growing	Viticoltura
Winemaking/Enology	Enologia
Enology/Winemaking	Enologia

English	Italian
Winery	Cantina
Wineskin/Bota Bag	Otre
Wire Cage/Muselet (For Champagne Corks)	Gabbietta
Yeast	Lieviti
Yellowish Red/Bricky	Con Riflessi Giallastri/ Mattonato
Bricky/Yellowish Red	Con Riflessi Giallastri/ Mattonato
Yield	Resa
Young	Giovane
Youth	Giovinezza
Zymurgy	Zimurgia

English - Spanish

English	Spanish
acescence	Acescencia
acetaldehyde	Acetaldehído
acetic	Acético
acetone	Acetona
acid	Ácido
acidic	Ácido
acidity	Acidez
acquired alcohol	alcohol adquirido
acrid	Acre
aerobic	Aerobio
aftertaste	Dejo
aftertaste	Resabio
aftertaste	Retrogusto
Aftertaste	Final de boca
age	Añejar
age (to)	Criar
aged	Añejado
aged	Añejo
aged wine	vino de guarda
aging	Envejecimiento
aging	Crianza

English	Spanish
agressive	Agresivo
albumin/egg white	Albúmina
alcohol	Alcohol
alcoholic	Alcóholico
alcoholic fermentation	fermentación alcohólica
alcoholization	Alcoholización
alcoholmeter	Alcohómetro
aldehyde	Aldehído
amber	Ámbar
amberish	Ambarino
angular	Aristas
animal	Animal
anthocyan	Antocian
anthocyanin	Antocianina
Appellation System (AVA)	Denominación de Origen Controlada (D.O.C)
aroma	Aroma
aromatic	Aromático
aromatic expression	Expresión aromática
astringency	Astringencia

English	Spanish
astringent	Astringente
attack	Ataque
attack	Entrada
austere	Austero
bakery	Pastelería
balance	Equilibrio
balance	Armonía
balanced	Equilibrado
Balling Degree	Grado de Balling
balsamic	Balsámico
barrel	Barrica
base wine	vino base
Bell Pepper	Pimiento morrón
berry	Grano
berry	Baya
beta-glucosidase	Beta-glucosidasa
big/generous wine	vino generoso
bitter	Amargo
bitter	amargo
bitterness	Amargor
bivarietal	Bivarietal

English	Spanish
black currant	Grosella negra
blanc de blancs	blanco de blancas
bland	Blando
blend	Corte
blend	Mezcla
bloom	Pruina
blue/iron casse	Quebradura férrica
botrytis cinerea (noble Rot)	podredumbre noble
botrytized	Botritizado
bottle	Embotellar
bottle-induced maceration	maceración inducida en botella
bottle-stink	Botella
bottled/bottling	Embotellado
bottling machine	Embotelladora
bouquet (tertiary aroma)	Bouquet
break the cap/punch down	Romper el sombrero
breathing	Respiración
brilliance	Brillantez

English	Spanish
brilliant	Brillante
brix degree	Brix (grado)
broken	Quebrado
brut	Brut
bucket	Cangilón (cadena de)
bulk wine	vino a granel
burnt	Quemado
butter	Mantequilla
buttery	Mantequilloso
cap	Sombrero
carafe	Garrafa
caramelized	Caramelizado
carbon dioxide	Anhídrido carbónico
carbonated	Gasificado
carbonic gas	Gas carbónico
carbonic maceration	maceración carbónica
carmine	Carmín
cask	Encubar
cask	Cuba
cask	Tonel
cask	Bordelesa

English	Spanish
casse	Quiebra
cassis	Casis
Caustic (Overly Sharp)	Mordiente
cedar	Cedro
cellar	Cava
centrifuge	Centrifugar
Champagne method	Método champenoise
chaptalization	Chaptalización
character	Carácter
Charmat method	Método charmat
cherry (sour)	Guinda
cherry (sweet)	Cereza
cherry red (color)	rojo cereza
chilled	Frappé
citrus	Cítrico
claret	Clarete
Clarify	Desborrar
Clarifying	Desborre
clarity	Claridad
clear	Limpio
closed	Cerrado

English	Spanish
clove	Clavo de olor
cloying	Empalagoso
cluster	Racimo
cold maceration	maceración en frío
colorimeter	Colorímetro
colouring material	Materia colorante
compact	Compacto
complex	Complejo
concentrated must	mosto concentrado
cool	Enfriar
cooled	Enfriado
cooper	Tonelero
cooper	Fabricar toneles
cooperage	Tonelería
cordon	Corona
cork	Corcho
cork taint (TCA)	Gusto a corcho
cream of tartar	Cremor tártaro
crisp	Vivaz
Crush/Grind	Moler
crusher	Estrujadora

English	Spanish
Crusher/Grinder	Moledora
crushing/Grinding	Molienda
crust/sediment	Costra
dates (fruit)	Dátiles
decant	Decantar
decanter	Decanter
Decanting	Decantado
decanting basket/cradle	Cesta
decanting cradle/basket	Cesta
decasked	Descubado
decasking	Descube
decrepit	Desvanecido
defective	Defectuoso
delicate	Delicado
demijohn	Damajuana
demisec	Demi-sec
deposit	Depósito
dessert/sweet wine	vino dulce
destem	Despalillar

English	Spanish
destemmer	Descobajadora
destemmer	Despalillador
destemming	Despalillado
destemming	Descobajado
developed	Desarrollado
developed	Evolucionado
Development notes	notas de evolución
dill	Eneldo
disgorge	Degollar
disgorgement	Degüello
distinctive	Distintivo
distinguished	Distinguido
Distributor	Expendedor
done	Listo
dosage	licor de expedición
drain	Escurrir
drainage	Drenado
drainers	Escurridor
dregs/lies	Borra
dried fruits	Frutos secos
dry	Seco

English	Spanish
earthy	Terroso
edge (on the)	Ribete
effervescence	Efervescencia
effervescent	Efervescente
egg white/albumin	Albúmina
egg whites	Clara de huevo
elegant	Elegante
enophile	Enófilo
enzyme	Enzima
estate	Finca
ester	Éster
ethanol	Etanol
ethereal	Etéreo
ethyl acetate	Acetato etílico
extract	Extracto
fat	Graso
feel	Toque
ferment	Fermentar
fermentation	Fermentación
fermentation trap	cuba de fermentación
filter	Filtrar

English	Spanish
filtering	Filtración
filtering	Filtrado
fine	Fino
fine (to clarify)	Clarificar
fining	Clarificación
finish	Acabado
finish (to)	Acabar
fire engine red	rojo fuego
firm	Firme
first press wine	vino de gota
flat	Flojo
flavor	Sabor
flavorful	Sabroso
Fleeting	Fugaz
Fleshy	Cuerpo
flexible	Flexible
flint	Grava
flinty	Pedernal
float	Flotar
floral	Floral
flute	Flauta

English	Spanish
foam	Espuma
fortified	Encabezado
fortified	Fortificado
fortified	Envinado
fortified wine	vino alcoholizado
fortified wine	vino fortificado
fortified wine	vino de licor
free-run juice	mosto flor
fresh	Fresco
fruity	Frutado
fruity	Frutal
full	Denso
full-bodied	Amplio
garlicy	Aliáceo
garnet-red	Granate
generic	Genérico
generous	Generoso
generous/big wine	vino generoso
geranium	Geranio
ginger	Jengibre
glucan	Glucano

English	Spanish
glycerin	Glicerina
glycerol	Glicerol
glycosidade	Glicosidasa
golden	Dorado
grape	Uva
grape seed	Pepita
grapefruit	Pomelo
grapevine	Vid
grassy/Herbacious	Herbáceo
green	Verde
green apples	Manzanas verdes
Green Wine	Vino verde
greenness/herbaceous	Verdor
Grind/Crush	Moler
Grinder/Crusher	Moledora
Grinding/crushing	Molienda
Grower	Cultivador
gum arabic	Goma arábiga
hard	Duro
harsh	Áspero
harvest (the)	Vendimia

English	Spanish
Harvest (to)	Cosecha
heady	Impetuoso
heavy	Pesado
herbaceous/greenness	Verdor
Herbacious/grassy	Herbáceo
highlights	Destello
highlights	Visos
hint	Nota
hogshead	Barril
hollow	Hueco
hopper	Tolva de descarga
horizontal shakers	Máquinas de sacudimiento horizonta
hose	Manguera
Hot (alcohol)	Puntas
hue	Tono
hue	Tinte
hue	Tonalidad
hues	Matices
icon wine	vino emblemático

English	Spanish
impoverished	Pobre
incense	Incienso
incisive	Incisivo
inky	Tinta china
insipid	Insípido
intense	Intenso
intensity	Intensidad
iron/blue casse	Quebradura férrica
jasmin	Jazmín
juice	Jugo
label	Etiqueta
lactic acid	ácido láctico
Lanolin	Lanolina
late	Tardío
late harvest	Cosecha tardía
leather	Cuero
lee	Madre
lees	Lías
legs/tears	Lágrima
light	Ligero
Limpidity	Limpidez

English	Spanish
lingering	Prolongado
liqueur de tirage (from French)	licor de tiraje
liquor	Licor
long	Largo
maceration	Maceración
maderized	Maderizado
Maderized (oxidized Aroma)	nariz oxidada
mahogany	Caoba
Main fermentation	Fermentación principal
malic	Málico
malic acid	ácido málico
malolactic casse	casse maloláctica
malolactic fermentation	fermentación maloláctica
maturation	Maduración
mature	Maduro
mature	Madurar
meager (lacking flavor)	Estirado
meaty	Carnoso
meniscus	Menisco

English	Spanish
menthol	Mentol
mentholated	Mentolado
middle palate	paladar medio
mineral	Mineral
minerality/mineral aromas	aromas minerales
Mineraly	notas minerales
mistelle	Mistela
mouthfeel	Tacto en boca
mucilage	Bozalado
muscat	Moscatel
muscat like	Amoscatelado
muselet/wire cage (for champagne corks)	Bozal
must	Mosto
naturally sweet	dulce natural
neck	Cuello
neck	Gollete
neutral	Neutro
new	Nuevo
new (nouveau) wine	vino del año

English	Spanish
noble Rot (botrytis cinerea)	podredumbre noble
nose	Nariz
nuances	Matices
nutmeg	nuez moscada
oak	Roble
oak chips	Chips
oak hints	notas de madera
oily	Oleoso
opalescent	Opalescente
opaque	Opaco
open	Abierto
orange peel	Cáscara de naranja
ordinary wine	vino ordinario
organoleptic	Organoléptico
Overwhelming/ Penetrating (aroma or taste)	Penetrante
oxidation	Oxidación
oxidative aging	crianza oxidativa
oxidized	Oxidado

English	Spanish
oxidized nose/ Maderized	nariz oxidada
pair	Maridar
pairing	Maridaje
palate	Paladar
pale	Pálido
paste like	Pastoso
pasteurization	Pasteurización
pasteurize	Pasteurizar
Penetrating/ Overwhelming (aroma or taste)	Penetrante
perfumed	Fragante
persistence	Persistencia
phenol	Fenol
phenolic	Fenólico
plum	Ciruela
polish (sandblast)	Arenar
polyphenol	Polifenol
pomace	Orujo
potassium bitartrate	Bitartrato de potasio
potential alcohol	alcohol potencial

English	Spanish
potentiality	Potencialidad
precipitant/sediment	Sedimentar
precipitate	Precipitar
precipitation	Precipitación
precipitation/ sedimentation	Sedimentación
premium	premio
premium wine	Gama
press (to)	Prensar
press wine	vino de prensa
pressing	Prensado
Pressings	Estrujado
Prickly (nose)	Punzante
producer	Productor
productive	Productivo
productivity	Productividad
pulp	Pulpa
pump over	Remontar
pumping	Bombeo
punch down/break the cap	Romper el sombrero

English	Spanish
purity	Pureza
purple	Púrpura
rack	Trasegar
racking	Trasiego
raisin wine	vino passito
raisining	Pasificación
raspberry	Frambuesa
recall	Recordar
rectified alcohol	alcohol rectificado
red	Rojo
red (for wine)	Tinto
red fruit	Frutos rojos
reduction	Reducción
reductive aromas	aromas de reducción
refractometer	Refractómetro
refractometry	Refractometría
refresh	Refrescar
reserve	Reserva
residual sugar	Azúcar residual
resin	Resina
rest	Reposar

English	Spanish
rest	Reposo
riddling	Remontaje
ripe skin	hollejo maduro
Robust	Corpulento
robust	Robusto
roller	Rodillo
rolling	Bastoneo
rolling	Bazuqueo
room temperature	Temperatura ambiente
rosé	Rosado
rotten egg	Huevos podridos
rough	Áspero
round	Redondo
roundness	Redondez
rubbery	Gomoso
ruby	Rubí
scales	Escala
secondary fermentation	fermentación secundaria
sediment	Sedimento
sediment/crust	Costra

English	Spanish
sediment/precipitant	Sedimentar
sedimentation/ precipitation	Sedimentación
seed	Semilla
serious	Serio
settle	Estacionar
settling (sediment)	Decantación
shaking table	Pupitre
sherrified/maderized	Ajerezado
sherrified/maderized	Ajerezado
shiny	Satinado
short time in barrel	fugaz paso por madera
Shredder	Trituradora
silky	Sedoso
singed	Rojizo
skin	Hollejo
slightly sparkling wine	vino de aguja
sluggish fermentation	fermentación lenta
smelling phase	Olfativo (fase)
smoky	Ahumado
soft	Suave

English	Spanish
softness	Suavidad
sound (not bad)	Franco
sparkling	Espumoso
sparkling wine	vino espumoso
spicy	Especiado
Spicy Hot	Picante
stabilisation	Estabilización
stabilise	Estabilizar
stable	Estable
stained	Manchado
stalk	Escobajo
stalk	Raspón
stave	Duela
stave/slat	Varilla
still wine	vino quieto
stirring up	Removido
stopper	tampone
storage	Almacenamiento
storage	Estiba
store	Estibar
straw (color)	Pajizo

English	Spanish
straw wine	vino passito
strawberry	Frutilla/Fresa
Strong	Fuerte
structure	Estructura
stuck fermentation	fermentación detenida
Substantial	Sustancioso
subtle	Sutil
succinic acid	ácido sucínico
sulfate	Sulfato
sulfited	Sulfitado
sulfurous	Sulfuroso
sulphur	Azufre
sulphur (to)	Azufrado
Sumptuous	Suntuoso
suspended solids	Partículas sólidas en suspensión
sweet	Abocado
sweet	Dulce
sweet/dessert wine	vino dulce
sweetness	Dulzor
syrup	Arrope

English	Spanish
syrupy	Licoroso
table grape	uva de mesa
table wine	vino de mesa
tank	Pileta
tank	Tanque
tannic	Tánico
tannin	Tanino
tap (on a barrel)	Canilla
tap (to tap barrel)	Espiche
tartaric acid	ácido tartárico
tartrate	Tartrato
taste	Degustar
taste (to)	Catar
taster	Catador
tasting (event)	Degustación
tasting (to be)	Cata
tasting phase	Gustativo
tenacity	Tenacidad
Tenderness	Tierno
terpene	Terpeno
terpenic	Terpénico

English	Spanish
terroir	Terruño
tertiary aroma (Bouquet)	Aroma terciario
texture	Textura
thin (lacking acid)	Delgado
toasted	Tostado
tobacco	Tabaco
total acidity	acidez total
total alcohol	alcohol total
Traditional Method	Método tradicional
transport	Acarreo
transport (to)	Acarrear
Tread (to press by foot)	pisada
tropical fruits	Frutas tropicales
truffle	Trufa
turbid	Turbio
turbidity	Turbidez
unbalanced	Desequilibrado
unctuous (overly sweet)	Untuoso
unripe berry	Agraz

English	Spanish
vanilla	Vainilla
vanilla	Avainillado
varietal	varietale
varietal wine	vino varietal
variety of vine/cultivar	Cepa
cultivar/variety of vine	Cepa
variety of Grape/cultivar	Variedad
cultivar/variety of Grape	Variedad
varnish	Barniz
vat	Vasija
velvety	Aterciopelado
vigorous	Vigoroso
vigorous fermentation	fermentación tumultuosa
vineyard	Viñedo
vinification/wine-making	Vinificación
vinous	Vinosidad
vintage (year)	Añada
violet (color)	Violáceo

English	Spanish
viscosity	Viscosidad
viscous	Viscoso
visual phase	Visual
Viticulture	Viticultura
volatile acidity	acidez volátil
voluptuous	Voluptuoso
walnut	Nuez
warm	Cálido
watery	Aguado
wet wool	Lana mojada
white	Blanco
white casse	Nube
wine	Vino
wine alcohol	alcohol vínico
wine in carafe	vino de jarra
wine pipe	Canuto
wine press	Lagar
wine press	Prensa
wine steward	Sommelier
wine tube/thief	Venencia/Venecia
winemaker/enologist	Enólogo

English	Spanish
enologist/winemaker	Enólogo
winemaking and grape growing	Vitivinicultura
winemaking/enology	Enología
enology/winemaking	Enología
winery	Bodega
wineskin/bota bag	Bota
wire cage/muselet (for champagne corks)	Bozal
yeast	Levadura
yellowish red/bricky	rojo amarillento
bricky/yellowish red	rojo amarillento
yield	Rendimiento
young	Joven
youth	Juventud
Zymurgy	Zymurgy

Spanish - English

Spanish	English
Abierto	Open
Abocado	Sweet
Acabado	Finish
Acabar	Finish (To)
Acarrear	Transport (To)
Acarreo	Transport
Acescencia	Acescence
Acetaldehído	Acetaldehyde
Acetato Etílico	Ethyl Acetate
Acético	Acetic
Acetona	Acetone
Acidez	Acidity
Acidez Total	Total Acidity
Acidez Volátil	Volatile Acidity
Ácido	Acid
Ácido	Acidic
Ácido Láctico	Lactic Acid
Ácido Málico	Malic Acid
Ácido Sucínico	Succinic Acid

Spanish	English
Ácido Tartárico	Tartaric Acid
Acre	Acrid
Aerobio	Aerobic
Agraz	Unripe Berry
Agresivo	Agressive
Aguado	Watery
Ahumado	Smoky
Ajerezado	Sherrified/Maderized
Ajerezado	Sherrified/Maderized
Albúmina	Albumin/Egg White
Albúmina	Egg White/Albumin
Alcohol	Alcohol
Alcohol Adquirido	Acquired Alcohol
Alcohol Potencial	Potential Alcohol
Alcohol Rectificado	Rectified Alcohol
Alcohol Total	Total Alcohol
Alcohol Vínico	Wine Alcohol
Alcóholico	Alcoholic
Alcoholización	Alcoholization

Spanish	English
Alcohómetro	Alcoholmeter
Aldehído	Aldehyde
Aliáceo	Garlicy
Almacenamiento	Storage
Amargo	Bitter
Amargo	Bitter
Amargor	Bitterness
Ámbar	Amber
Ambarino	Amberish
Amoscatelado	Muscat Like
Amplio	Full-Bodied
Añada	Vintage (Year)
Añejado	Aged
Añejar	Age
Añejo	Aged
Anhídrido Carbónico	Carbon Dioxide
Animal	Animal
Antocian	Anthocyan
Antocianina	Anthocyanin

Spanish	English
Arenar	Polish (Sandblast)
Aristas	Angular
Armonía	Balance
Aroma	Aroma
Aroma Terciario	Tertiary Aroma (Bouquet)
Aromas De Reducción	Reductive Aromas
Aromas Minerales	Minerality/Mineral Aromas
Aromático	Aromatic
Arrope	Syrup
Áspero	Harsh
Áspero	Rough
Astringencia	Astringency
Astringente	Astringent
Ataque	Attack
Aterciopelado	Velvety
Austero	Austere
Avainillado	Vanilla
Azúcar Residual	Residual Sugar

Spanish	English
Azufrado	Sulphur (To)
Azufre	Sulphur
Balsámico	Balsamic
Barniz	Varnish
Barrica	Barrel
Barril	Hogshead
Bastoneo	Rolling
Baya	Berry
Bazuqueo	Rolling
Beta-Glucosidasa	Beta-Glucosidase
Bitartrato De Potasio	Potassium Bitartrate
Bivarietal	Bivarietal
Blanco	White
Blanco De Blancas	Blanc De Blancs
Blando	Bland
Bodega	Winery
Bombeo	Pumping
Bordelesa	Cask
Borra	Dregs/Lies

Spanish	English
Bota	Wineskin/Bota Bag
Botella	Bottle-Stink
Botritizado	Botrytized
Bouquet	Bouquet (Tertiary Aroma)
Bozal	Muselet/Wire Cage (For Champagne Corks)
Bozal	Wire Cage/Muselet (For Champagne Corks)
Bozalado	Mucilage
Brillante	Brilliant
Brillantez	Brilliance
Brix (Grado)	Brix Degree
Brut	Brut
Cálido	Warm
Cangilón (Cadena De)	Bucket
Canilla	Tap (On A Barrel)
Canuto	Wine Pipe
Caoba	Mahogany

Spanish	English
Carácter	Character
Caramelizado	Caramelized
Carmín	Carmine
Carnoso	Meaty
Cáscara De Naranja	Orange Peel
Casis	Cassis
Casse Maloláctica	Malolactic Casse
Cata	Tasting (To Be)
Catador	Taster
Catar	Taste (To)
Cava	Cellar
Cedro	Cedar
Centrifugar	Centrifuge
Cepa	Variety Of Vine/Cultivar
Cepa	Cultivar/Variety Of Vine
Cereza	Cherry (Sweet)
Cerrado	Closed
Cesta	Decanting Basket/ Cradle

Spanish	English
Cesta	Decanting Cradle/ Basket
Chaptalización	Chaptalization
Chips	Oak Chips
Ciruela	Plum
Cítrico	Citrus
Clara De Huevo	Egg Whites
Clarete	Claret
Claridad	Clarity
Clarificación	Fining
Clarificar	Fine (To Clarify)
Clavo De Olor	Clove
Colorímetro	Colorimeter
Compacto	Compact
Complejo	Complex
Corcho	Cork
Corona	Cordon
Corpulento	Robust
Corte	Blend

Spanish	English
Cosecha	Harvest (To)
Cosecha Tardía	Late Harvest
Costra	Crust/Sediment
Costra	Sediment/Crust
Cremor Tártaro	Cream Of Tartar
Crianza	Aging
Crianza Oxidativa	Oxidative Aging
Criar	Age (To)
Cuba	Cask
Cuba De Fermentación	Fermentation Trap
Cuello	Neck
Cuero	Leather
Cuerpo	Fleshy
Cultivador	Grower
Damajuana	Demijohn
Dátiles	Dates (Fruit)
Decantación	Settling (Sediment)
Decantado	Decanting
Decantar	Decant

Spanish	English
Decanter	Decanter
Defectuoso	Defective
Degollar	Disgorge
Degüello	Disgorgement
Degustación	Tasting (Event)
Degustar	Taste
Dejo	Aftertaste
Delgado	Thin (Lacking Acid)
Delicado	Delicate
Demi-Sec	Demisec
Denominación De Origen Controlada (D.O.C)	Appellation System (Ava)
Denso	Full
Depósito	Deposit
Desarrollado	Developed
Desborrar	Clarify
Desborre	Clarifying
Descobajado	Destemming
Descobajadora	Destemmer

Spanish	English
Descubado	Decasked
Descube	Decasking
Desequilibrado	Unbalanced
Despalillado	Destemming
Despalillador	Destemmer
Despalillar	Destem
Destello	Highlights
Desvanecido	Decrepit
Distinguido	Distinguished
Distintivo	Distinctive
Dorado	Golden
Drenado	Drainage
Duela	Stave
Dulce	Sweet
Dulce Natural	Naturally Sweet
Dulzor	Sweetness
Duro	Hard
Efervescencia	Effervescence
Efervescente	Effervescent

Spanish	English
Elegante	Elegant
Embotellado	Bottled/Bottling
Embotelladora	Bottling Machine
Embotellar	Bottle
Empalagoso	Cloying
Encabezado	Fortified
Encubar	Cask
Eneldo	Dill
Enfriado	Cooled
Enfriar	Cool
Enófilo	Enophile
Enología	Winemaking/Enology
Enología	Enology/Winemaking
Enólogo	Winemaker/Enologist
Enólogo	Enologist/Winemaker
Entrada	Attack
Envejecimiento	Aging
Envinado	Fortified
Enzima	Enzyme

Spanish	English
Equilibrado	Balanced
Equilibrio	Balance
Escala	Scales
Escobajo	Stalk
Escurridor	Drainers
Escurrir	Drain
Especiado	Spicy
Espiche	Tap (To Tap Barrel)
Espuma	Foam
Espumoso	Sparkling
Estabilización	Stabilisation
Estabilizar	Stabilise
Estable	Stable
Estacionar	Settle
Éster	Ester
Estiba	Storage
Estibar	Store
Estirado	Meager (Lacking Flavor)

Spanish	English
Estructura	Structure
Estrujado	Pressings
Estrujadora	Crusher
Etanol	Ethanol
Etéreo	Ethereal
Etiqueta	Label
Evolucionado	Developed
Expendedor	Distributor
Expresión Aromática	Aromatic Expression
Extracto	Extract
Fabricar Toneles	Cooper
Fenol	Phenol
Fenólico	Phenolic
Fermentación	Fermentation
Fermentación Alcohólica	Alcoholic Fermentation
Fermentación Detenida	Stuck Fermentation
Fermentación Lenta	Sluggish Fermentation

Spanish	English
Fermentación Maloláctica	Malolactic Fermentation
Fermentación Principal	Main Fermentation
Fermentación Secundaria	Secondary Fermentation
Fermentación Tumultuosa	Vigorous Fermentation
Fermentar	Ferment
Filtración	Filtering
Filtrado	Filtering
Filtrar	Filter
Final De Boca	Aftertaste
Finca	Estate
Fino	Fine
Firme	Firm
Flauta	Flute
Flexible	Flexible
Flojo	Flat
Floral	Floral
Flotar	Float

Spanish	English
Fortificado	Fortified
Fragante	Perfumed
Frambuesa	Raspberry
Franco	Sound (Not Bad)
Frappé	Chilled
Fresco	Fresh
Frutado	Fruity
Frutal	Fruity
Frutas Tropicales	Tropical Fruits
Frutilla/Fresa	Strawberry
Frutos Rojos	Red Fruit
Frutos Secos	Dried Fruits
Fuerte	Strong
Fugaz	Fleeting
Fugaz Paso Por Madera	Short Time In Barrel
Gama	Premium Wine
Garrafa	Carafe
Gas Carbónico	Carbonic Gas

Spanish	English
Gasificado	Carbonated
Genérico	Generic
Generoso	Generous
Geranio	Geranium
Glicerina	Glycerin
Glicerol	Glycerol
Glicosidasa	Glycosidade
Glucano	Glucan
Gollete	Neck
Goma Arábiga	Gum Arabic
Gomoso	Rubbery
Grado De Balling	Balling Degree
Granate	Garnet-Red
Grano	Berry
Graso	Fat
Grava	Flint
Grosella Negra	Black Currant
Guinda	Cherry (Sour)
Gustativo	Tasting Phase

Spanish	English
Gusto A Corcho	Cork Taint (Tca)
Herbáceo	Grassy/Herbacious
Herbáceo	Herbacious/Grassy
Hollejo	Skin
Hollejo Maduro	Ripe Skin
Hueco	Hollow
Huevos Podridos	Rotten Egg
Impetuoso	Heady
Incienso	Incense
Incisivo	Incisive
Insípido	Insipid
Intensidad	Intensity
Intenso	Intense
Jazmín	Jasmin
Jengibre	Ginger
Joven	Young
Jugo	Juice
Juventud	Youth
Lagar	Wine Press

Spanish	English
Lágrima	Legs/Tears
Lana Mojada	Wet Wool
Lanolina	Lanolin
Largo	Long
Levadura	Yeast
Lías	Lees
Licor	Liquor
Licor De Expedición	Dosage
Licor De Tiraje	Liqueur De Tirage (From French)
Licoroso	Syrupy
Ligero	Light
Limpidez	Limpidity
Limpio	Clear
Listo	Done
Maceración	Maceration
Maceración Carbónica	Carbonic Maceration
Maceración En Frío	Cold Maceration
Maceración Inducida En Botella	Bottle-Induced Maceration

Spanish	English
Maderizado	Maderized
Madre	Lee
Maduración	Maturation
Madurar	Mature
Maduro	Mature
Málico	Malic
Manchado	Stained
Manguera	Hose
Mantequilla	Butter
Mantequilloso	Buttery
Manzanas Verdes	Green Apples
Máquinas De Sacudimiento Horizonta	Horizontal Shakers
Maridaje	Pairing
Maridar	Pair
Materia Colorante	Colouring Material
Matices	Hues
Matices	Nuances
Menisco	Meniscus

Spanish	English
Mentol	Menthol
Mentolado	Mentholated
Método Champenoise	Champagne Method
Método Charmat	Charmat Method
Método Tradicional	Traditional Method
Mezcla	Blend
Mineral	Mineral
Mistela	Mistelle
Moledora	Crusher/Grinder
Moledora	Grinder/Crusher
Moler	Crush/Grind
Moler	Grind/Crush
Molienda	Crushing/Grinding
Molienda	Grinding/Crushing
Mordiente	Caustic (Overly Sharp)
Moscatel	Muscat
Mosto	Must
Mosto Concentrado	Concentrated Must
Mosto Flor	Free-Run Juice

Spanish	English
Nariz	Nose
Nariz Oxidada	Maderized (Oxidized Aroma)
Nariz Oxidada	Oxidized Nose/ Maderized
Neutro	Neutral
Nota	Hint
Notas De Evolución	Development Notes
Notas De Madera	Oak Hints
Notas Minerales	Mineraly
Nube	White Casse
Nuevo	New
Nuez	Walnut
Nuez Moscada	Nutmeg
Oleoso	Oily
Olfativo (Fase)	Smelling Phase
Opaco	Opaque
Opalescente	Opalescent
Organoléptico	Organoleptic
Orujo	Pomace

Spanish	English
Oxidación	Oxidation
Oxidado	Oxidized
Pajizo	Straw (Color)
Paladar	Palate
Paladar Medio	Middle Palate
Pálido	Pale
Partículas Sólidas En Suspensión	Suspended Solids
Pasificación	Raisining
Pastelería	Bakery
Pasteurización	Pasteurization
Pasteurizar	Pasteurize
Pastoso	Paste Like
Pedernal	Flinty
Penetrante	Overwhelming/ Penetrating (Aroma Or Taste)
Penetrante	Penetrating/ Overwhelming (Aroma Or Taste)
Pepita	Grape Seed

Spanish	English
Persistencia	Persistence
Pesado	Heavy
Picante	Spicy Hot
Pileta	Tank
Pimiento Morrón	Bell Pepper
Pisada	Tread (To Press By Foot)
Pobre	Impoverished
Podredumbre Noble	Botrytis Cinerea (Noble Rot)
Podredumbre Noble	Noble Rot (Botrytis Cinerea)
Polifenol	Polyphenol
Pomelo	Grapefruit
Potencialidad	Potentiality
Precipitación	Precipitation
Precipitar	Precipitate
Premio	Premium
Prensa	Wine Press
Prensado	Pressing

Spanish	English
Prensar	Press (To)
Productividad	Productivity
Productivo	Productive
Productor	Producer
Prolongado	Lingering
Pruina	Bloom
Pulpa	Pulp
Puntas	Hot (Alcohol)
Punzante	Prickly (Nose)
Pupitre	Shaking Table
Pureza	Purity
Púrpura	Purple
Quebrado	Broken
Quebradura Férrica	Blue/Iron Casse
Quebradura Férrica	Iron/Blue Casse
Quemado	Burnt
Quiebra	Casse
Racimo	Cluster
Raspón	Stalk

Spanish	English
Recordar	Recall
Redondez	Roundness
Redondo	Round
Reducción	Reduction
Refractometría	Refractometry
Refractómetro	Refractometer
Refrescar	Refresh
Remontaje	Riddling
Remontar	Pump Over
Removido	Stirring Up
Rendimiento	Yield
Reposar	Rest
Reposo	Rest
Resabio	Aftertaste
Reserva	Reserve
Resina	Resin
Respiración	Breathing
Retrogusto	Aftertaste
Ribete	Edge (On The)

Spanish	English
Roble	Oak
Robusto	Robust
Rodillo	Roller
Rojizo	Singed
Rojo	Red
Rojo Amarillento	Yellowish Red/Bricky
Rojo Amarillento	Bricky/Yellowish Red
Rojo Cereza	Cherry Red (Color)
Rojo Fuego	Fire Engine Red
Romper El Sombrero	Break The Cap/Punch Down
Romper El Sombrero	Punch Down/Break The Cap
Rosado	Rosé
Rubí	Ruby
Sabor	Flavor
Sabroso	Flavorful
Satinado	Shiny
Seco	Dry

Spanish	English
Sedimentación	Precipitation/ Sedimentation
Sedimentación	Sedimentation/ Precipitation
Sedimentar	Precipitant/Sediment
Sedimentar	Sediment/Precipitant
Sedimento	Sediment
Sedoso	Silky
Semilla	Seed
Serio	Serious
Sombrero	Cap
Sommelier	Wine Steward
Suave	Soft
Suavidad	Softness
Sulfato	Sulfate
Sulfitado	Sulfited
Sulfuroso	Sulfurous
Suntuoso	Sumptuous
Sustancioso	Substantial
Sutil	Subtle

Spanish	English
Tabaco	Tobacco
Tacto En Boca	Mouthfeel
Tampone	Stopper
Tánico	Tannic
Tanino	Tannin
Tanque	Tank
Tardío	Late
Tartrato	Tartrate
Temperatura Ambiente	Room Temperature
Tenacidad	Tenacity
Terpénico	Terpenic
Terpeno	Terpene
Terroso	Earthy
Terruño	Terroir
Textura	Texture
Tierno	Tenderness
Tinta China	Inky
Tinte	Hue
Tinto	Red (For Wine)

Spanish	English
Tolva De Descarga	Hopper
Tonalidad	Hue
Tonel	Cask
Tonelería	Cooperage
Tonelero	Cooper
Tono	Hue
Toque	Feel
Tostado	Toasted
Trasegar	Rack
Trasiego	Racking
Trituradora	Shredder
Trufa	Truffle
Turbidez	Turbidity
Turbio	Turbid
Untuoso	Unctuous (Overly Sweet)
Uva	Grape
Uva De Mesa	Table Grape
Vainilla	Vanilla

Spanish	English
Variedad	Variety Of Grape/Cultivar
Variedad	Cultivar/Variety Of Grape
Varietale	Varietal
Varilla	Stave/Slat
Vasija	Vat
Vendimia	Harvest (The)
Venencia/Venecia	Wine Tube/Thief
Verde	Green
Verdor	Greenness/Herbaceous
Verdor	Herbaceous/Greenness
Vid	Grapevine
Vigoroso	Vigorous
Viñedo	Vineyard
Vinificación	Vinification/Wine-Making
Vino	Wine
Vino A Granel	Bulk Wine

Spanish	English
Vino Alcoholizado	Fortified Wine
Vino Base	Base Wine
Vino De Aguja	Slightly Sparkling Wine
Vino De Gota	First Press Wine
Vino De Guarda	Aged Wine
Vino De Jarra	Wine In Carafe
Vino De Licor	Fortified Wine
Vino De Mesa	Table Wine
Vino De Prensa	Press Wine
Vino Del Año	New (Nouveau) Wine
Vino Dulce	Dessert/Sweet Wine
Vino Dulce	Sweet/Dessert Wine
Vino Emblemático	Icon Wine
Vino Espumoso	Sparkling Wine
Vino Fortificado	Fortified Wine
Vino Generoso	Big/Generous Wine
Vino Generoso	Generous/Big Wine
Vino Ordinario	Ordinary Wine
Vino Passito	Raisin Wine

Spanish	English
Vino Passito	Straw Wine
Vino Quieto	Still Wine
Vino Varietal	Varietal Wine
Vino Verde	Green Wine
Vinosidad	Vinous
Violáceo	Violet (Color)
Viscosidad	Viscosity
Viscoso	Viscous
Visos	Highlights
Visual	Visual Phase
Viticultura	Viticulture
Vitivinicultura	Winemaking And Grape Growing
Vivaz	Crisp
Voluptuoso	Voluptuous
Zymurgy	Zymurgy

Italian - English

Italian	English
Fabbrica Di Botte	Cooperage
Vino Frizzante	Slightly Sparkling Wine
Abbocato	Sweet
Acerbità	Greenness/ Herbaceous
Acerbità	Herbaceous/ Greenness
Acescenza	Acescence
Acetaldeide	Acetaldehyde
Acetato Di Etile	Ethyl Acetate
Acetone	Acetone
Acidità	Acidity
Acidità Totale	Total Acidity
Acidità Volatile	Volatile Acidity
Acido	Acid
Acido Lattico	Lactic Acid
Acido Malico	Malic Acid
Acido Succinico	Succinic Acid
Acido Tartarico	Tartaric Acid
Acino	Berry
Acre	Acrid

Italian	English
Aerobico	Aerobic
Affumicato	Smoky
Aggiunto Di Moscato	Muscat Like
Aggressivo	Agressive
Agitazione	Rolling
Albumina	Albumin/Egg White
Albumina	Egg White/Albumin
Alcol	Alcohol
Alcol Arricchito	Acquired Alcohol
Alcol Potenziale	Potential Alcohol
Alcol Rettificato	Rectified Alcohol
Alcol Totale	Total Alcohol
Alcol Vinico	Wine Alcohol
Alcolizzato Vino	Fortified Wine
Alcoolato	Alcoholic
Alcoolizzazione	Alcoholization
Aldeide	Aldehyde
Allevare	Age (To)
Allungato	Lingering
Amarena	Cherry (Sour)
Amaro	Bitter

Italian	English
Amaro	Bitter
Amaro	Bitterness
Ambra	Amber
Ambrato	Amberish
Ampio	Full-Bodied
Aneto	Dill
Angoli	Angular
Animale	Animal
Annacquato	Watery
Annacquato/Aggiunto Di	Meager (Lacking Flavor)
Annata	Vintage (Year)
Antocianina	Anthocyanin
Antociano	Anthocyan
Aperto	Open
Appasimento	Raisining
Armonia	Balance
Aroma	Aroma
Aroma Terziario	Tertiary Aroma (Bouquet)
Aromatico	Aromatic

Italian	English
Arome Minerali	Minerality/Mineral Aromas
Arricchito	Fortified
Aspro	Harsh
Aspro	Rough
Assaggio	Tasting (Event)
Assagiare	Taste
Astringente	Astringent
Astringenza	Astringency
Attacco	Attack
Austero	Austere
Avvinato	Fortified
Azienda Agricola	Estate
Bacchetta	Stave/Slat
Balsamico	Balsamic
Banco Mobile	Shaking Table
Barile	Barrel
Barile	Hogshead
Barile/Barrica	Cask
Bastonatura	Rolling

Italian	English
Battistrada	Tread (To Press By Foot)
Ben Freddo	Chilled
Beta-Glucoside	Beta-Glucosidase
Bianco	White
Bianco D'uovo/Chiaro D'uovo	Egg Whites
Biossido Di Carbonio	Carbon Dioxide
Bitartrato Di Potasio	Potassium Bitartrate
Bivarietale	Bivarietal
Blanc De Blancs	Blanc De Blancs
Botritizzata	Botrytized
Bottaio	Cooper
Botte	Cask
Botte	Cask
Bottiglia (Puzza Di)	Bottle-Stink
Brillante	Brilliant
Brillantezza	Brilliance
Brix	Brix Degree
Bruciato(Sapore/ Gusto)	Burnt
Brut	Brut

Italian	English
Buccia	Skin
Buccia Di Arancia	Orange Peel
Buccia Matura	Ripe Skin
Buco	Hollow
Burro	Butter
Burroso	Buttery
Caloroso	Warm
Cannuccia	Wine Pipe
Cantina	Cellar
Cantina	Winery
Capello	Cap
Caraffa/Bombola	Carafe
Caramellato	Caramelized
Carattere	Character
Carnoso	Meaty
Cedro	Cedar
Centrifugare	Centrifuge
Ceppo	Tap (To Tap Barrel)
Ceppo	Variety Of Vine/Cultivar
Ceppo	Cultivar/Variety Of Vine

Italian	English
Cesta	Decanting Basket/ Cradle
Cesta	Decanting Cradle/ Basket
Chiarezza	Clarity
Chiarifica	Clarifying
Chiarifica	Fining
Chiarificare	Clarify
Chiarificare	Fine (To Clarify)
Chiodi Di Garofano	Clove
Chips/Segatura	Oak Chips
Chiuso	Closed
Ciliegia	Cherry (Sweet)
Citrico	Citrus
Claretto	Claret
Collo	Neck
Colorato/Rosso	Red (For Wine)
Colorimetro	Colorimeter
Coltivatore	Grower
Compatto	Compact
Competitivo	Premium

Italian	English
Complesso	Complex
Complesso/Corposo	Velvety
Con Corpo	Fleshy
Con Riflessi Giallastri/ Mattonato	Yellowish Red/Bricky
Con Riflessi Giallastri/ Mattonato	Bricky/Yellowish Red
Con Riflessi Rossi	Singed
Conservazione	Aging
Conservazione In Fase Ossidante	Oxidative Aging
Contenitore Di Fermentazione	Fermentation Trap
Corona	Cordon
Cremor Tartaro	Cream Of Tartar
Crosta	Crust/Sediment
Crosta	Sediment/Crust
Cuoio	Leather
Damigiana	Demijohn
Datteri	Dates (Fruit)
Debole/Molle	Flat
Decantato	Decanting

Italian	English
Decantatore/Brocca	Decanter
Degustare	Taste (To)
Degustatore	Taster
Degustatore	Wine Tube/Thief
Degustatore/ Consigliere/Sommelier	Wine Steward
Degustazione	Tasting (To Be)
Delicato	Delicate
Demi-Sec	Demisec
Denominazione Di Origine Controllata	Appellation System (Ava)
Denso	Full
Deposito	Deposit
Difettoso	Defective
Diraspare	Destem
Diraspato	Destemming
Diraspatura	Destemmer
Diraspatura	Destemmer
Diraspatura	Destemming
Disrapare/Pigliare	Crush/Grind
Disrapare/Pigliare	Grind/Crush

Italian	English
Distintivo	Distinctive
Distributore	Distributor
Doga	Stave
Dolce	Sweet
Dolce Naturale	Naturally Sweet
Dolcezza	Sweetness
Dorato	Golden
Drenato	Drainage
Duro	Green Wine
Duro	Hard
Duro	Unripe Berry
Effervescente	Effervescent
Effervescenza	Effervescence
Elegante	Elegant
Eme	Seed
Enofilo	Enophile
Enologia	Winemaking/Enology
Enologia	Enology/Winemaking
Enologo	Winemaker/Enologist
Enologo	Enologist/Winemaker
Enzima	Enzyme

Italian	English
Equilibrato	Balanced
Equilibrio	Balance
Erbaceo	Grassy/Herbacious
Erbaceo	Herbacious/Grassy
Espressione Aromatica	Aromatic Expression
Estere	Ester
Estratto	Extract
Etanolo	Ethanol
Etereo	Ethereal
Etichetta	Label
Etilometro	Alcoholmeter
Evole	Cloying
Evoluto	Developed
Fabbricare Botti	Cooper
Fase Olfattiva	Smelling Phase
Fatto	Done
Feccia/Sedimento	Dregs/Lies
Fenolico	Phenolic
Fenolo	Phenol
Fermentare	Ferment
Fermentazione	Fermentation

Italian	English
Fermentazione Alcolica	Alcoholic Fermentation
Fermentazione Ferrica	Blue/Iron Casse
Fermentazione Ferrica	Iron/Blue Casse
Fermentazione Incompleta	Stuck Fermentation
Fermentazione Interrotta/Malolattica	Malolactic Casse
Fermentazione Lenta	Sluggish Fermentation
Fermentazione Malolattica	Malolactic Fermentation
Fermentazione Principale	Main Fermentation
Fermentazione Secondaria	Secondary Fermentation
Fermentazione Tumultuosa	Vigorous Fermentation
Filtraggio	Filtering
Filtrare	Filter
Filtrato	Filtering
Finale Di Bocca	Aftertaste
Finito/Pieno	Finish
Fino	Fine
Flessibile	Flexible

Italian	English
Floreale	Floral
Flute	Flute
Forte	Strong
Fragola	Strawberry
Fragrante	Perfumed
Franco/Genuino	Sound (Not Bad)
Fresco	Fresh
Frutato	Fruity
Frutato	Fruity
Frutta Secca	Dried Fruits
Frutti Di Bosco	Red Fruit
Frutti Tropicali	Tropical Fruits
Fugace	Fleeting
Fumature	Highlights
Fune	Lees
Gabbietta	Muselet/Wire Cage (For Champagne Corks)
Gabbietta	Wire Cage/Muselet (For Champagne Corks)
Galleggiare	Float

Italian	English
Gamma	Premium Wine
Gas Carbonico	Carbonic Gas
Gassoso	Carbonated
Gelsomino	Jasmin
Generico	Generic
Generoso	Generous
Geranio	Geranium
Ghiaia	Flint
Giovane	Young
Giovinezza	Youth
Glicerina	Glycerin
Glicerolo	Glycerol
Gluconato	Glucan
Glucosidasi	Glycosidade
Gomma Arabica	Gum Arabic
Gommoso	Rubbery
Grado Di Ballo	Balling Degree
Granata	Garnet-Red
Grano	Berry
Grappolo	Cluster
Grasso	Fat

Italian	English
Grondatore	Drainers
Gustativa	Tasting Phase
Imbottare	Cask
Imbottigliare	Bottle
Imbottigliato	Bottled/Bottling
Imbottigliatrice	Bottling Machine
Immagazzinaggio	Storage
Immagazzinamento	Storage
Immagazzinare	Store
Impetuoso	Heady
Incenso	Incense
Inchiostro	Hue
Inchiostro	Inky
Incisivo	Incisive
Ingabbiettatura	Mucilage
Ingzolforato	Sulphur (To)
Inizio	Attack
Insieme Di Profumi	Bouquet (Tertiary Aroma)
Insipido	Insipid
Intensità	Intensity

Italian	English
Intenso	Intense
Invecchiamento	Aging
Invecchiare	Age
Invecchiare	Settle
Invecchiato	Aged
Invecchiato	Aged
Lacrime/Archetti	Legs/Tears
Lampone	Raspberry
Lana Bagnata	Wet Wool
Lanolina	Lanolin
Leggero	Light
Lieviti	Yeast
Limpidezza	Limpidity
Liqueur De Tirage	Liqueur De Tirage (From French)
Liquore	Liquor
Liquore Di Spedizione	Dosage
Liquoroso	Syrupy
Lungo	Long
Macchiato	Stained

Italian	English
Macchina A Scuotimento Orizontale	Horizontal Shakers
Macerazione	Maceration
Macerazione A Freddo	Cold Maceration
Macerazione Carbonica	Carbonic Maceration
Macerazione Indotta In Bottiglia	Bottle-Induced Maceration
Maderizzato/Marsalato	Maderized
Madre	Lee
Magro	Thin (Lacking Acid)
Malico	Malic
Marciume Nobile	Botrytis Cinerea (Noble Rot)
Marciume Nobile	Noble Rot (Botrytis Cinerea)
Marsalato	Sherrified/Maderized
Marsalato	Sherrified/Maderized
Materia Colorante	Colouring Material
Matrimonio	Pairing
Maturare	Mature
Maturazione	Maturation

Italian	English
Maturo	Mature
Mele Verdi	Green Apples
Menisco	Meniscus
Mentolo	Menthol
Mentolo	Mentholated
Mescolare	Pair
Metodo Classico	Champagne Method
Metodo In Autoclave	Charmat Method
Metodo Tradizionale	Traditional Method
Mezzo Palato	Middle Palate
Minerale	Mineral
Mistella	Mistelle
Mogano	Mahogany
Molle	Bland
Morbidezza	Softness
Mordente	Caustic (Overly Sharp)
Moscato	Muscat
Mosto	Must
Mosto Concentrato	Concentrated Must
Mosto Fiore	Free-Run Juice
Nec	Neck

Italian	English
Neutro	Neutral
Nobile/Austero	Distinguished
Noce	Walnut
Noce Moscata	Nutmeg
Nota	Edge (On The)
Nota	Hint
Nuovo	New
Nuvola	White Casse
Oddore Di Aglio	Garlicy
Oleoso	Oily
Opaco	Opaque
Opalescente	Opalescent
Organolettico	Organoleptic
Ossidato	Oxidized
Ossidazione	Oxidation
Otre	Wineskin/Bota Bag
Paglierino	Straw (Color)
Palato	Palate
Pallido	Pale
Particelle Solide In Sospensione	Suspended Solids

Italian	English
Passagio Veloce Per Il Legno	Short Time In Barrel
Pasticceria	Bakery
Pastorizzare	Pasteurize
Pastorizzazione	Pasteurization
Pastoso	Paste Like
Penetrante	Overwhelming/ Penetrating (Aroma Or Taste)
Penetrante	Penetrating/ Overwhelming (Aroma Or Taste)
Peperone Dolce	Bell Pepper
Persistenza/Tenacita	Persistence
Pesante	Heavy
Pezzo Di Terra	Terroir
Piccante	Spicy Hot
Pietra Fuocaia/Selce	Flinty
Pigiatrice	Crusher
Pigliatrice	Crusher/Grinder
Pigliatrice	Grinder/Crusher
Pigliatura	Crushing/Grinding
Pigliatura	Grinding/Crushing

Italian	English
Polifenolo	Polyphenol
Polpa	Pulp
Pompaggio	Pumping
Pompelmo	Grapefruit
Porpora	Purple
Potenzialità	Potentiality
Povero	Impoverished
Precipitare	Precipitant/Sediment
Precipitare	Precipitate
Precipitare	Sediment/Precipitant
Precipitato	Sediment
Precipitazione	Precipitation
Premitura	Pressings
Pressa	Wine Press
Pressare	Press (To)
Pressatura	Pressing
Prima Sensazione Di Fumo Di Alcool	Hot (Alcohol)
Produttività	Productivity
Produttivo	Productive
Produttore	Producer

Italian	English
Profumo/Odore/Sapore	Nose
Pruina	Bloom
Pruna/Susina	Plum
Pulito	Clear
Pungente	Acetic
Pungente	Prickly (Nose)
Purezza	Purity
Raccolto	Harvest (To)
Raffreddare	Cool
Raffreddato	Cooled
Raspo	Stalk
Recipiente	Vat
Resa	Yield
Resina	Resin
Respirazione	Breathing
Retrogusto	Aftertaste
Retrogusto	Aftertaste
Retrogusto	Aftertaste
Ribes Nero	Black Currant
Ribes Nero	Cassis

Italian	English
Ricordare	Recall
Riduzione	Reduction
Rifractometria	Refractometry
Rifrattometro	Refractometer
Rimontaggio	Riddling
Rimontare	Pump Over
Rimosso	Stirring Up
Rimuovere Dalla Botte	Decasked
Rinforzato	Fortified
Rinfrescare	Refresh
Riposare	Rest
Riposo	Rest
Riserva	Reserve
Robusto	Robust
Robusto	Robust
Rompere Il Cappello Di Fermentazione	Break The Cap/Punch Down
Rompere Il Cappello Di Fermentazione	Punch Down/Break The Cap
Rosato	Rosé
Rosso	Red

Italian	English
Rosso Carmine	Carmine
Rosso Ciliegia	Cherry Red (Color)
Rosso Fuoco	Fire Engine Red
Rotondità	Roundness
Rotondo	Round
Rotto	Broken
Rottura	Casse
Rovere/Quercia (Sapore)	Oak
Rubinetto	Tap (On A Barrel)
Rubino	Ruby
Rullo	Roller
Ruvideza	Stalk
Sabbiare	Polish (Sandblast)
Sapore	Flavor
Sapore D'uovo Marchio	Rotten Egg
Sapore Di Ossidato	Maderized (Oxidized Aroma)
Sapore Di Ossidato	Oxidized Nose/ Maderized
Sapore Di Ridotto	Reductive Aromas

Italian	English
Sapore Di Sughero	Cork Taint (Tca)
Sapore Di Vaniglia	Vanilla
Saporoso	Flavorful
Satinato	Shiny
Sboccatura	Disgorgement
Scala	Scales
Sciroppo	Syrup
Secchio	Bucket
Secco	Dry
Sedimentazione/ Precipitazione	Precipitation/ Sedimentation
Sedimentazione/ Precipitazione	Sedimentation/ Precipitation
Sensazione Organolettica	Mouthfeel
Separare	Decant
Separazione	Settling (Sediment)
Serbatoio	Tank
Serio	Serious
Setoso	Silky
Sfumature	Hues
Sfumature	Nuances

Italian	English
Sgozzare/Aprire	Disgorge
Sgrondare	Drain
Solfato	Sulfate
Solfitato	Sulfited
Solforoso	Sulfurous
Solidità	Texture
Solido	Firm
Sontuoso	Sumptuous
Sostanzioso	Substantial
Sottile	Subtle
Speziato	Spicy
Spuma	Foam
Spumante	Sparkling
Squilibrato	Unbalanced
Stabile	Stable
Stabilizzare	Stabilise
Stabilizzazione	Stabilisation
Stati Di Evoluzione	Development Notes
Struttura	Structure
Suave/Morbido	Soft
Succo	Juice

Italian	English
Svanito	Decrepit
Sviluppato/Non Sviluppato	Developed
Svinatura	Decasking
Tabacco	Tobacco
Taglio	Blend
Taglio	Blend
Tampón	Stopper
Tannicco	Tannic
Tannino	Tannin
Tappo	Cork
Tardivo	Late
Tartrato	Tartrate
Tartufo	Truffle
Temperatura Ambiente	Room Temperature
Tenacia	Tenacity
Tenero	Tenderness
Terminare	Finish (To)
Terpenico	Terpenic
Terpeno	Terpene
Terroso	Earthy

Italian	English
Tocchi Di Legno	Oak Hints
Tocchi Minerali	Mineraly
Tocco	Feel
Tonalità	Hue
Tono	Hue
Torbidezza	Turbidity
Torbido	Turbid
Tostato	Toasted
Tramoggia	Wine Press
Tramoggia Di Scarico	Hopper
Trasportare	Transport (To)
Trasporto	Transport
Travasare	Rack
Travaso	Racking
Trituratrice	Shredder
Tubo Flessibile	Hose
Ulousacido	Acidic
Untuoso	Unctuous (Overly Sweet)
Uva	Grape
Uva Da Tavola	Table Grape

Italian	English
Vaniglia	Vanilla
Varietà	Variety Of Grape/Cultivar
Varietà	Cultivar/Variety Of Grape
Varietal	Varietal
Vasca	Tank
Vendemmia	Harvest (The)
Vendemmia Tardiva	Late Harvest
Verde	Green
Vernice	Varnish
Vigneto	Vineyard
Vigoroso	Vigorous
Vinaccia	Pomace
Vinacciolo	Grape Seed
Vinificazione	Vinification/Wine-Making
Vino	Wine
Vino Base	Base Wine
Vino Da Tavola	Table Wine
Vino Dell'annata	New (Nouveau) Wine

Italian	English
Vino Destinato Al Invecchiamento	Aged Wine
Vino Di Aggiunto	Fortified Wine
Vino Di Laccrima	First Press Wine
Vino Di Pressa/Torchio	Press Wine
Vino Dolce	Dessert/Sweet Wine
Vino Dolce	Sweet/Dessert Wine
Vino Emblematico	Icon Wine
Vino Fermo	Still Wine
Vino Generoso	Big/Generous Wine
Vino Generoso	Generous/Big Wine
Vino Liquoroso	Fortified Wine
Vino Passito	Raisin Wine
Vino Passito	Straw Wine
Vino Senza Qualità	Ordinary Wine
Vino Sfuso	Bulk Wine
Vino Sfuso/In Caraffa	Wine In Carafe
Vino Spumante	Sparkling Wine
Vino Varietale	Varietal Wine
Vinosità	Vinous
Violaceo	Violet (Color)

Italian	English
Viscosita	Viscosity
Viscoso	Viscous
Visiva	Visual Phase
Vite	Grapevine
Viticoltura	Viticulture
Viticoltura	Winemaking And Grape Growing
Vivace	Crisp
Vivacità/Brillantezza	Highlights
Voluttuoso	Voluptuous
Zenzero	Ginger
Zimurgia	Zymurgy
Zolfo	Sulphur
Zuccheraggio	Chaptalization
Zucchero Residuo	Residual Sugar

German - English

German	English
Abstichmethode	Charmat Method
Apfelaroma	Green Apples
Etikett	Label
Vanille	Vanilla
Versandlikör	Dosage
Viskozität	Viscosity
Weinbau	Viticulture
Abbeeren	Destemming
Abbeeren/Entrappen	Destem
Abbeermaschine	Destemmer
Abfüllen	Bottle
Abfüllmaschine	Bottling Machine
Abgelagert	Aged
Abgelagert	Aged
Abkühlen	Cool
Ablagern	Age
Ablagern	Rest
Abpumpen	Pumping
Abstechen	Decasking

German	English
Abstechen/Entleeren	Rack
Abtropfbrett	Drainers
Acetaldehyd	Acetaldehyde
Adstringierend	Astringent
Adstringierender Effekt	Astringency
Aerob	Aerobic
Aldehyd	Aldehyde
Alkohol	Alcohol
Alkoholisch	Alcoholic
Alkoholische Gärung	Alcoholic Fermentation
Alkoholometer	Alcoholmeter
Alkoholreich	Syrupy
Alkoholzusatz	Alcoholization
Alkolholzusatz	Fortified
Alter Von Wein	Aged Wine
Alterung	Aging
Alterungsprozess Oxidation	Oxidative Aging
Amber	Amber

German	English
Anämisch	Open
Anstich	Tap (To Tap Barrel)
Anthocyane	Anthocyanin
Apfel-Milchsäure-Gärung	Malolactic Fermentation
Apfelgeschmack	Malic
Apfelsäure	Malic Acid
Arm	Impoverished
Aroma	Aroma
Aroma Nach Karamel	Caramelized
Aromatisch	Aromatic
Aromatischer Ausdruck	Aromatic Expression
Aromen Reduktion	Reductive Aromas
Artig	Tenderness
Äthanol	Ethanol
Ätherisch	Ethereal
Aufbrausen	Effervescence
Aufgeblüht	Developed

German	English
Aufsteigend/ Aufdringlich	Overwhelming/ Penetrating (Aroma Or Taste)
Aufsteigend/ Aufdringlich	Penetrating/ Overwhelming (Aroma Or Taste)
Ausbau	Stabilisation
Ausfällen	Precipitate
Ausgebaut	Finish
Ausgeglichen	Balanced
Ausgeglichenheit	Balance
Ausgereift	Done
Ausgespritet	Fortified
Ausgleichen	Stabilise
Auspressen	Pressings
Ausspeien	Disgorge
Austrieb	Clarifying
Bäckerei	Bakery
Balling-Grade	Balling Degree
Balsamisch	Balsamic

German	English
Beere	Berry
Beere	Berry
Beerenaroma	Red Fruit
Beerenhautmazeration	Cold Maceration
Beerenhülse	Skin
Befall	Attack
Beginn	Attack
Bernsteinfarben/ Topasfarben/ Bernsteingelb	Amberish
Betha-Glucosidase	Beta-Glucosidase
Bissig	Caustic (Overly Sharp)
Bitter	Bitter
Bitterkeit	Bitterness
Bitterlich	Bitter
Blanc	Blanc De Blancs
Blauwerden	Blue/Iron Casse
Blauwerden	Iron/Blue Casse
Bleich	Pale

German	English
Blumenblau	Anthocyan
Blütenduft	Floral
Boden	Terroir
Bodengeschmack	Earthy
Bodensatz	Dregs/Lies
Böttchermeister	Cooper
Bottich	Tank
Brenzlig/Brandiges Aroma	Burnt
Brix-Grade	Brix Degree
Bruch	Casse
Brut	Brut
Bügelverschluss	Muselet/Wire Cage (For Champagne Corks)
Bügelverschluss	Wire Cage/Muselet (For Champagne Corks)
Bukett	Bouquet (Tertiary Aroma)
Butter	Butter
Butterig	Buttery

German	English
Chaptalizierung	Chaptalization
Charakter	Character
Compac	Compact
Dattel	Dates (Fruit)
Dauben	Stave
Dekantieren	Decant
Dekantieren	Settling (Sediment)
Dekantierkörbchen	Decanting Basket/ Cradle
Dekantierkörbchen	Decanting Cradle/ Basket
Dekantiert	Decanting
Delikat	Delicate
Depot	Sediment
Depot Bilden	Precipitant/Sediment
Depot Bilden	Sediment/Precipitant
Depot Bildung	Precipitation/ Sedimentation
Depot Bildung	Sedimentation/ Precipitation
Dicht	Full

German	English
Dill	Dill
Dränage	Drainage
Duftend	Perfumed
Eckig/Kantig	Hot (Alcohol)
Edelfäule	Botrytis Cinerea (Noble Rot)
Edelfäule	Noble Rot (Botrytis Cinerea)
Eiche	Oak
Eichen-Chips	Oak Chips
Eimerkette	Bucket
Einfach	Ordinary Wine
Einfach	Wine In Carafe
Einlagern	Cask
Eiweiß	Albumin/Egg White
Eiweiß	Egg White/Albumin
Eiweiß	Egg Whites
Elegant	Elegant
Ende	Finish (To)
Eng Verbinden	Pair

German	English
Enge Verbindung	Pairing
Enthefung	Disgorgement
Entkapselt	Decasked
Entkorken	Break The Cap/Punch Down
Entkorken	Punch Down/Break The Cap
Entleerung	Racking
Entsaften	Drain
Entwässerung Saft	Free-Run Juice
Entwickelt	Developed
Entwicklungshinweise	Development Notes
Enzym	Enzyme
Erdbeere	Strawberry
Ergiebig	Productive
Erinnern	Recall
Ernst	Austere
Ernst	Serious
Ernte	Harvest (To)
Erntemaschine	Horizontal Shakers

German	English
Ertrag	Yield
Erzeuger	Grower
Erzeuger	Producer
Essigsäureäthylester	Ethyl Acetate
Essigstich	Acescence
Ester	Ester
Extrakt	Extract
Fad	Bland
Fad	Insipid
Farbdepot	Crust/Sediment
Farbdepot	Sediment/Crust
Farbstoff	Colouring Material
Farbton	Hue
Färbung	Hues
Fass	Cask
Fass	Cask
Fass	Hogshead
Fassbestand	Cooperage
Fasshahn	Tap (On A Barrel)

German	English
Faule Eier	Rotten Egg
Fehlerhaft	Defective
Fein	Fine
Feiner Tischwein	Big/Generous Wine
Feiner Tischwein	Generous/Big Wine
Fest	Firm
Fett	Fat
Feuchte Wolle	Wet Wool
Feuersteingeschmack	Flinty
Feurig/Feurigrot	Fire Engine Red
Filtern	Filter
Filtern	Filtering
Firnis	Varnish
Flach	Flat
Flasche	Bottle-Stink
Flaschenfüllung	Bottled/Bottling
Flaschengärungverfahren	Champagne Method
Flaschenhals	Neck

German	English
Flaschenhals	Neck
Fleischig	Meaty
Flexibel	Flexible
Flüchtig	Fleeting
Flüchtige	Volatile Acidity
Frisch	Fresh
Fruchtfleisch	Pulp
Fruchtig	Fruity
Fruchtig/Obstig	Fruity
Fuchsrot	Singed
Füllig	Full-Bodied
Funke	Highlights
Gärbehälter	Fermentation Trap
Gären/Säuern	Ferment
Gärung	Fermentation
Gärung Verhaftet	Stuck Fermentation
Gattungsbezeichnung	Generic
Gaumen	Palate
Gefäß/Behälte	Vat

German	English
Gefiltert	Filtering
Geharzt	Resin
Gekühlt	Chilled
Gelbliches Rot	Yellowish Red/Bricky
Gelbliches Rot	Bricky/Yellowish Red
Generös	Generous
Geranie	Geranium
Geräuchert	Smoky
Gerbstoff	Tannin
Geröstet	Toasted
Gesamtalkohol	Total Alcohol
Gesamtsäure	Total Acidity
Geschmack	Flavor
Geschmacklich	Tasting Phase
Geschmeidig	Unctuous (Overly Sweet)
Gespriteter Wein	Fortified Wine
Gespriteter Wein	Fortified Wine
Getrübt	Broken

German	English
Gewürznelke	Clove
Glanz	Brilliance
Glänzend	Brilliant
Glucan	Glucan
Glykosidase	Glycosidade
Glyzerin	Glycerin
Glyzerol	Glycerol
Goldgelb	Golden
Granatfarben	Garnet-Red
Grasig/Grasherb	Grassy/Herbacious
Grasig/Grasherb	Herbacious/Grassy
Grün	Green
Grundwein	Base Wine
Grüngeschmack	Greenness/Herbaceous
Grüngeschmack	Herbaceous/Greenness
Gummi Arabicum	Gum Arabic
Gummiartig	Rubbery
Halbtrocken	Demisec

German	English
Harmonie	Balance
Hart	Hard
Hart	Harsh
Hart	Rough
Hauch	Feel
Hauptgärung	Main Fermentation
Hauptteilwein	Bulk Wine
Hefe	Yeast
Herkunftsbezeichnung	Appellation System (Ava)
Herzhaft	Heady
Himbeere	Raspberry
Hochfein	Subtle
Hochreif	Late
Holzgeschmack	Oak Hints
Ikonischen Wein	Icon Wine
Ingwer	Ginger
Intensität	Intensity
Jahrgang	Vintage (Year)

German	English
Jasmin	Jasmin
Jugend	Youth
Jung	Young
Kaliumbitartrat	Potassium Bitartrate
Kaltgärung	Sluggish Fermentation
Kantig	Angular
Kapsel	Cap
Karaffe	Carafe
Karaffe	Decanter
Karminrot	Carmine
Kelter	Crusher/Grinder
Kelter	Grinder/Crusher
Keltern	Crush/Grind
Keltern	Grind/Crush
Keltern	Pressing
Kelterung	Crushing/Grinding
Kelterung	Grinding/Crushing
Kern	Grape Seed
Kern	Seed

German	English
Keton	Acetone
Kiesgrund	Flint
Kirsche	Cherry (Sweet)
Kirschrot	Cherry Red (Color)
Klären	Settle
Klarettwein	Claret
Klarheit	Clarity
Klarheit	Limpidity
Klärung/Schönung	Fining
Kleines Fass	Barrel
Knoblaucharoma	Garlicy
Kohlendyoxid/ Kohlensäure	Carbonic Gas
Kohlensäure	Carbon Dioxide
Kohlensäurehaltige Mazeration	Carbonic Maceration
Kolorimeter	Colorimeter
Komplex	Complex
Konzentrierter Most	Syrup
Korbflasche	Demijohn

German	English
Kork	Cork
Korkgeschmack	Cork Taint (Tca)
Körperreich	Fleshy
Körperreich	Robust
Kosten/Probieren	Taste
Kraft	Potentiality
Küpfermeister	Cooper
Kurze Zeit In Holz	Short Time In Barrel
Lager	Rest
Lagern	Storage
Lang	Lingering
Lanoline	Lanolin
Latte/Leiste	Stave/Slat
Laufen Wein	First Press Wine
Laufffläche	Tread (To Press By Foot)
Lebhaft	Crisp
Lecker	Flavorful
Lederflasche	Wineskin/Bota Bag

German	English
Ledergeruch	Leather
Leer	Hollow
Leicht	Light
Leicht Säuerlich	Acrid
Likör	Liquor
Likörartig	Liqueur De Tirage (From French)
Likörwein	Fortified Wine
Lüftung	Breathing
Maderisiert	Maderized
Mager/Dünn	Thin (Lacking Acid)
Mahagonibaum	Mahogany
Manna	Unripe Berry
Mazerierung	Maceration
Mazerierung In Der Flasche	Bottle-Induced Maceration
Meniskus	Meniscus
Menthol	Menthol
Milchsäure	Lactic Acid
Milde	Softness

German	English
Mineralisch	Mineral
Mineralisch	Mineraly
Mineralisches Aroma	Minerality/Mineral Aromas
Mischpult	Shaking Table
Mistela	Mistelle
Mit Kohlensäure	Carbonated
Mit Menthol	Mentholated
Mitte Gaumen	Middle Palate
Most	Must
Mostigsüß/Pappsüß/ Widerlich Süß	Cloying
Mostkonzentrat	Concentrated Must
Muselage	Mucilage
Muskatbukett/ Muskattellerton	Muscat Like
Muskateller	Muscat
Muskatnuss	Nutmeg
Nachgärung	Secondary Fermentation
Nachgeschmack	Aftertaste

German	English
Nachgeschmack	Aftertaste
Nachgescmack	Aftertaste
Nachhalt	Tenacity
Nachhaltig	Long
Nachhaltigkeit	Persistence
Nachwirkend	Aftertaste
Nase	Nose
Natursüße	Naturally Sweet
Neuer Wein	New
Neuer Wein	New (Nouveau) Wine
Neutral	Neutral
Niederschlag	Deposit
Niederschlag	Precipitation
Note	Edge (On The)
Note	Hint
Nuance	Nuances
Nussgeschmack	Dried Fruits
Oenophil	Enophile
Ohne Bodensatz	Clarify

German	English
Olfaktorisch	Smelling Phase
Ölig	Oily
Önologe	Winemaker/Enologist
Önologe	Enologist/Winemaker
Önologie	Winemaking/Enology
Önologie	Enology/Winemaking
Opalisierend	Opalescent
Orangenschale	Orange Peel
Organoleptisch	Organoleptic
Organoleptische Empfindung	Mouthfeel
Oxidierte Nase	Maderized (Oxidized Aroma)
Oxidierte Nase	Oxidized Nose/ Maderized
Oxidierung	Oxidation
Pampelmuse	Grapefruit
Paprika	Bell Pepper
Pasteurisieren	Pasteurization
Pasteurisieren	Pasteurize

German	English
Perlwein	Slightly Sparkling Wine
Pflaume	Plum
Pfropfen	Stopper
Phenol	Phenol
Phenolisch	Phenolic
Poliphenole	Polyphenol
Potentiell Vorhandener Alkohol	Potential Alcohol
Prachtvoll	Sumptuous
Premiumwein	Premium
Presse	Wine Press
Presse	Wine Press
Pressen	Press (To)
Probezieher/ Weinheber	Wine Tube/Thief
Produktivität	Productivity
Purpurfarben	Purple
Quebradura Maloláctica	Malolactic Casse
Quetschmaschine	Shredder

German	English
Rappe	Stalk
Rappen	Stalk
Rauh	Agressive
Raumtemperatur	Room Temperature
Rebsorte	Varietal
Rebsorte	Variety Of Vine/Cultivar
Rebsorte	Cultivar/Variety Of Vine
Rebsorte	Variety Of Grape/Cultivar
Rebsorte	Cultivar/Variety Of Grape
Reduktion	Reduction
Refraktometer	Refractometer
Refraktometrie	Refractometry
Reif	Bloom
Reif	Mature
Reif/Gereift	Mature
Reife	Lee
Reife Beerenhülse	Ripe Skin
Reifen	Maturation

German	English
Reinheit	Purity
Reintönig	Sound (Not Bad)
Rektifizierter Alkohol	Rectified Alcohol
Reserve	Reserve
Restzucker	Residual Sugar
Robust/Solid	Robust
Rolle	Roller
Roséwein	Rosé
Rosinen	Raisining
Rot	Red
Rotwein	Red (For Wine)
Rubin	Ruby
Rund	Round
Rundung	Roundness
Rütteln	Riddling
Saft	Juice
Samtig	Velvety
Sandeln	Polish (Sandblast)
Sanft/Geschmeidig	Soft

German	English
Sauber	Clear
Sauerkirsche	Cherry (Sour)
Säuerlich	Acidic
Säure	Acid
Säuregehalt	Acidity
Schal	Decrepit
Scharf	Prickly (Nose)
Scharf	Spicy Hot
Schaum	Foam
Schaumkrone	Cordon
Schaumwein	Sparkling
Schaumwein	Sparkling Wine
Scheitermost	Press Wine
Schillern	Highlights
Schimmelbefall	Botrytized
Schlagen/Umrühren	Rolling
Schlauch	Hose
Schneide Den Traubenstiel	Destemming

German	English
Schneidig	Incisive
Schönen/Klären	Fine (To Clarify)
Schwarze Johannisbeere	Black Currant
Schwarze Johannisbeere	Cassis
Schwebstoffe	Suspended Solids
Schwefel	Sulphur
Schwefeln	Sulphur (To)
Schwer	Heavy
Schwimmen	Float
Seidig	Shiny
Seidig	Silky
Sektglas	Flute
Sherrygeschmack	Sherrified/Maderized
Sherrygeschmack	Sherrified/Maderized
Sich Unterscheiden	Distinctive
Sommelier	Wine Steward
Spätlese	Late Harvest
Spitzenwein	Premium Wine

German	English
Spritzig/Prickeln	Effervescent
Stabil	Stable
Staffelung	Scales
Stapeln	Store
Stark	Strong
Stauung	Storage
Stichig	Acetic
Stillwein	Still Wine
Strohfarben	Straw (Color)
Strohwein	Raisin Wine
Strohwein	Straw Wine
Struktur	Structure
Struktur	Texture
Stürmische Gärung	Vigorous Fermentation
Succinsäure	Succinic Acid
Sulfat	Sulfate
Sulfidisch/ Schwefelhaltig	Sulfurous
Süß	Sweet

German	English
Süß	Sweet
Süße	Sweetness
Süßwein	Dessert/Sweet Wine
Süßwein	Sweet/Dessert Wine
Tabak	Tobacco
Tafeltrauben	Table Grape
Tank	Tank
Tanninhaltig	Tannic
Tartrat	Tartrate
Tatsächlich Entwickelter Alkohol	Acquired Alcohol
Terpene	Terpene
Terpenisch	Terpenic
Tertiäres Aroma	Tertiary Aroma (Bouquet)
Tiefgekühlt	Cooled
Tieraroma	Animal
Tinte	Inky
Tischwein/Tafelwein	Table Wine
Ton	Hue

German	English
Tonne	Cask
Tönung	Hue
Traditionelle Methode	Traditional Method
Träne	Legs/Tears
Transport	Transport
Transportieren	Transport (To)
Traube	Cluster
Traube	Grape
Traubenabbeermaschine	Destemmer
Traubenernte	Harvest (The)
Traubenmühle	Crusher
Trester	Pomace
Trocken	Dry
Trogförmiger Trichter Der Traubenmühle	Hopper
Tropenfrüchte	Tropical Fruits
Trub	Lees
Trüb	Turbid
Trübschleier	Turbidity

German	English
Trüffel	Truffle
Tube	Wine Pipe
Überschwefelt	Sulfited
Überstreckt	Meager (Lacking Flavor)
Umpumpen	Pump Over
Umrühren	Stirring Up
Unausgewogen	Unbalanced
Undurchsichtig	Opaque
Unreif	Closed
Unterstoßen	Rolling
Vanillegeschmack/ Vanilleduft	Vanilla
Verfärbt	Stained
Verjüngen	Refresh
Verjus	Green Wine
Verkäufer	Distributor
Verkosten	Taste (To)
Verschnitt	Blend
Verschnitt	Blend

German	English
Verschnitt	Varietal Wine
Verschnitten	Bivarietal
Versiedet/Oxidiert	Oxidized
Verstärkt	Fortified
Violett	Violet (Color)
Visuelle	Visual Phase
Vollkommen	Voluptuous
Vollmundig/Körperreich	Intense
Vollmundig/Körperreich	Substantial
Vornehm	Distinguished
Walnuss	Walnut
Wärmend	Warm
Wässerig	Watery
Weihrauchgeruch	Incense
Wein	Wine
Weinalkohol	Wine Alcohol
Weinbau	Winemaking And Grape Growing
Weinbaugebiet	Vineyard

German	English
Weinbereitung	Vinification/Wine-Making
Weingut	Estate
Weinig	Vinous
Weinkeller	Cellar
Weinkeller	Winery
Weinpflege	Aging
Weinprobe	Tasting (Event)
Weinprobe/Weinkost	Tasting (To Be)
Weinsäure	Tartaric Acid
Weinstein	Cream Of Tartar
Weinstock	Grapevine
Weinverkoster	Taster
Weisser Bruch	White Casse
Weißwein	White
Widerstandsfähig	Vigorous
Würzig	Spicy
Zähflüssig	Paste Like
Zähflüssig	Viscous

German	English
Zeder	Cedar
Zentrifugieren	Centrifuge
Zitrusfrucht	Citrus
Züchten	Age (To)
Zymurgie	Zymurgy

French - English

French	English
Abocado	Sweet
Acajou	Mahogany
Acerbe	Bitter
Acescence	Acescence
Acétaldéhyde	Acetaldehyde
Acétate D'éthyle	Ethyl Acetate
Acétique	Acetic
Acétone	Acetone
Acide	Acid
Acide	Acidic
Acide Lactique	Lactic Acid
Acide Malique	Malic Acid
Acide Succinique	Succinic Acid
Acide Tartrique	Tartaric Acid
Acidité	Acidity
Acidité Totale	Total Acidity
Acidité Volatile	Volatile Acidity
Âcre	Acrid
Aérobie	Aerobic
Agressif	Agressive

French	English
Aigu	Prickly (Nose)
Albumine	Albumin/Egg White
Albumine	Egg White/Albumin
Alcool	Alcohol
Alcool Acquis	Acquired Alcohol
Alcool De Prestations Viniques	Wine Alcohol
Alcool En Puissance/ Alcool Potentiel	Potential Alcohol
Alcool Rectifié	Rectified Alcohol
Alcool Total	Total Alcohol
Alcooleux	Alcoholic
Alcoolisation	Alcoholization
Alcoomètre	Alcoholmeter
Aldéhyde	Aldehyde
Ambre	Amber
Ambré	Amberish
Amer	Bitter
Amer/Amertume	Bitterness
Ample	Full-Bodied
Aneth	Dill

French	English
Anhydride Carbonique	Carbon Dioxide
Animal	Animal
Anthocyane	Anthocyan
Anthocyanine	Anthocyanin
Appellation D'origine Contrôlée	Appellation System (Ava)
Arête	Angular
Aromatique	Aromatic
Arôme	Aroma
Arôme Tertiaire	Tertiary Aroma (Bouquet)
Arômes De Réduction	Reductive Aromas
Arômes Minéraux	Minerality/Mineral Aromas
Arrière-Goût	Aftertaste
Arrière-Goût	Aftertaste
Arrière-Goût	Aftertaste
Assemblage	Blend
Astringence	Astringency
Astringent	Astringent
Attaque	Attack

French	English
Attaque	Attack
Austère	Austere
Aviné	Fortified
Baguette	Stave/Slat
Baie	Berry
Balsamique	Balsamic
Baril	Hogshead
Barrique	Barrel
Bâtonnage	Rolling
Beta-Glucosidase	Beta-Glucosidase
Beurre	Butter
Beurré	Buttery
Bitartrate De Potassium	Potassium Bitartrate
Blanc	White
Blanc D'œuf	Egg Whites
Blanc De Blancs	Blanc De Blancs
Boisé	Maderized
Bonbonne	Carafe
Bordelaise	Cask
Botrytisé	Botrytized

French	English
Bouchon	Cork
Bouchon	Stopper
Bouquet	Bouquet (Tertiary Aroma)
Bouteille (Puanteur De)	Bottle-Stink
Brillance	Brilliance
Brillant	Brilliant
Broyeur	Shredder
Brûlé	Burnt
Brut	Brut
Caractère	Character
Carafe	Decanter
Caramélisé	Caramelized
Carmin	Carmine
Casse	Casse
Cassé	Broken
Casse Blanche	White Casse
Casse Ferrique	Blue/Iron Casse
Casse Ferrique	Iron/Blue Casse
Casse Malolactique	Malolactic Casse

French	English
Casser Le Chapeau	Break The Cap/Punch Down
Casser Le Chapeau	Punch Down/Break The Cap
Cassis	Black Currant
Cassis	Cassis
Cave	Cellar
Cave	Winery
Cèdre	Cedar
Centrifuger	Centrifuge
Cep	Variety Of Vine/Cultivar
Cep	Cultivar/Variety Of Vine
Cépage	Variety Of Grape/Cultivar
Cépage	Cultivar/Variety Of Grape
Cerise	Cherry (Sweet)
Chapeau	Cap
Chaptalisation	Chaptalization
Charnu	Meaty
Chaud	Warm
Chêne	Oak

French	English
Cigare/Tabac	Tobacco
Citrique	Citrus
Clairet	Claret
Clarification	Fining
Clarifier	Fine (To Clarify)
Clarté	Clarity
Clou De Girofle	Clove
Colorimètre	Colorimeter
Compact	Compact
Complexe	Complex
Conquet	Hopper
Copeaux De Bois	Oak Chips
Cordon	Cordon
Corpulent	Fleshy
Corpulent	Robust
Coupage/Mélange	Blend
Crème De Tartre	Cream Of Tartar
Cuir	Leather
Cuve	Cask
Cuve	Tank

French	English
Cuve	Tank
Cuve	Vat
Cuve De Fermentation	Fermentation Trap
Dame-Jeanne	Demijohn
Dates	Dates (Fruit)
Débitant	Distributor
Débourrement	Clarifying
Débourrer	Clarify
Décantation	Settling (Sediment)
Décanté	Decanting
Décanter	Decant
Décharné/Maigre	Thin (Lacking Acid)
Décuvage	Decasking
Décuvé	Decasked
Défectueux	Defective
Dégorgeage	Disgorgement
Dégorger	Disgorge
Degré Balling	Balling Degree
Degré Brix	Brix Degree
Dégustateur	Taster

French	English
Dégustateur	Wine Tube/Thief
Dégustation	Tasting (Event)
Dégustation	Tasting (To Be)
Déguster	Taste
Déguster	Taste (To)
Délicat	Delicate
Demi-Sec	Demisec
Dense	Full
Déposer/Sédimenter	Precipitant/Sediment
Déposer/Sédimenter	Sediment/Precipitant
Dépôt	Deposit
Dépôt En Croûte	Crust/Sediment
Dépôt En Croûte	Sediment/Crust
Dépôt/Sédimentation	Precipitation/Sedimentation
Dépôt/Sédimentation	Sedimentation/Precipitation
Déséquilibré	Unbalanced
Deux Cépages	Bivarietal
Distinctif	Distinctive
Distingué	Distinguished

French	English
Domaine/Propriété	Estate
Doré	Golden
Douceur	Softness
Douceur	Sweetness
Douceur Naturelle	Naturally Sweet
Douelle	Stave
Doux	Sweet
Drainage	Drainage
Dur	Hard
Dur	Harsh
Dur	Rough
Échelle	Scales
Écœurant	Cloying
Effervescence	Effervescence
Effervescent	Effervescent
Égoutter	Drain
Égouttoir	Drainers
Égrappage/Éraflage	Destemming
Égrappé	Destemming
Égrapper	Destem

French	English
Égrappoir	Destemmer
Élégant	Elegant
Élevage	Aging
Élevage Oxydatif	Oxidative Aging
Élever	Age (To)
Embouteiller/Mettre En Bouteilles	Bottle
Emmagasinage	Storage
Emmagasiner	Store
En Fin De Bouche	Aftertaste
Encens	Incense
Encre De Chine	Inky
Enfoncement Du Chapeau	Rolling
Enzyme	Enzyme
Épanoui	Developed
Épicé	Spicy
Équilibre	Balance
Équilibré	Balanced
Érafloir	Destemmer
Ester	Ester

French	English
Éthanol	Ethanol
Éthéré	Ethereal
Étiquette	Label
Étoffé	Balance
Éventé	Decrepit
Évolué	Developed
Expression Aromatique	Aromatic Expression
Extrait	Extract
Fabriquer Des Fûts/ Tonellerie	Cooper
Faible	Flat
Fait	Done
Ferme	Firm
Fermentation	Fermentation
Fermentation Alcoolique	Alcoholic Fermentation
Fermentation Arrêtée/ Suspendue	Stuck Fermentation
Fermentation Lente	Sluggish Fermentation
Fermentation Malolactique	Malolactic Fermentation

French	English
Fermentation Principale	Main Fermentation
Fermentation Tumultueuse	Vigorous Fermentation
Fermenter	Ferment
Filtrage	Filtering
Filtration	Filtering
Filtrer	Filter
Fin	Fine
Fini	Finish
Finir	Finish (To)
Flexible/Souple	Flexible
Floral	Floral
Flotter	Float
Flûte	Flute
Fort	Strong
Fortifié	Fortified
Fortifié	Fortified
Foulage	Crushing/Grinding
Foulage	Grinding/Crushing
Foulé	Pressings

French	English
Fouler	Crush/Grind
Fouler	Grind/Crush
Fouler	Tread (To Press By Foot)
Fouloir	Crusher
Fouloir	Crusher/Grinder
Fouloir	Grinder/Crusher
Frais/Fraîche	Fresh
Fraise	Strawberry
Framboise	Raspberry
Franc	Sound (Not Bad)
Frappé	Chilled
Frappé	Cooled
Frapper	Cool
Fruité	Fruity
Fruité	Fruity
Fruits Rouges	Red Fruit
Fruits Secs	Dried Fruits
Fruits Tropicaux	Tropical Fruits
Fugace	Fleeting
Fumé	Smoky

French	English
Fût	Cask
Gamme	Premium Wine
Gaz Carbonique	Carbonic Gas
Gazéifié	Carbonated
Généreux	Generous
Générique	Generic
Géranium	Geranium
Gingembre	Ginger
Glucane	Glucan
Glycérine	Glycerin
Glycérol	Glycerol
Glycosidase	Glycosidade
Godets	Bucket
Gomme Arabique	Gum Arabic
Gommeux	Rubbery
Goulot/Cou	Neck
Goulot/Cou	Neck
Goût De Bouchon	Cork Taint (Tca)
Goût De Pierre À Fusil	Flinty
Grain	Berry

French	English
Grappe	Cluster
Gras	Fat
Graves	Flint
Grenat	Garnet-Red
Grillé	Toasted
Griotte	Cherry (Sour)
Gustatif	Tasting Phase
Herbacé	Grassy/Herbacious
Herbacé	Herbacious/Grassy
Huileux	Oily
Impétueux	Heady
Incisif	Incisive
Insipide	Insipid
Intense	Intense
Intensité	Intensity
Jambe/Larme	Legs/Tears
Jasmin	Jasmin
Jeune	Young
Jeunesse	Youth
Jus	Juice

French	English
Jus D'égouttage/Jus De Goutte	Free-Run Juice
Laine Mouillée	Wet Wool
Laisser Reposer	Settle
Lanoline	Lanolin
Léger	Light
Léger Passage En Bois/En Barrique	Short Time In Barrel
Levure	Yeast
Lie	Dregs/Lies
Lie	Lees
Lie (De Vin)	Lee
Limpidité	Limpidity
Liqueur	Liquor
Liqueur D'expédition	Dosage
Liqueur De Tirage	Liqueur De Tirage (From French)
Liquoreux	Syrupy
Liséré	Edge (On The)
Loger	Cask
Long	Long

French	English
Longue/Prolongé	Lingering
Lourd	Heavy
Macération	Maceration
Macération À Froid	Cold Maceration
Macération Carbonique	Carbonic Maceration
Macération Induite En Bouteille	Bottle-Induced Maceration
Machine À Embouteiller	Bottling Machine
Machine À Vendanger	Horizontal Shakers
Malique	Malic
Manne	Unripe Berry
Marc	Pomace
Mariage	Pairing
Marier	Pair
Matière Colorante	Colouring Material
Maturation	Maturation
Méchage/Soufré	Sulphur (To)
Ménisque	Meniscus
Menthol	Menthol

French	English
Mentholé	Mentholated
Méthode Champenoise	Champagne Method
Méthode Charmat	Charmat Method
Méthode Traditionnelle	Traditional Method
Milieu De Bouche	Middle Palate
Millésime	Vintage (Year)
Minéral	Mineral
Mise En Bouteilles	Bottled/Bottling
Mistelle	Mistelle
Mœlleux/Qui A De La Substance	Substantial
Mordant	Caustic (Overly Sharp)
Mou	Bland
Mouillée	Watery
Mousse	Foam
Mousseux	Sparkling
Moût	Must
Moût Concentré	Concentrated Must
Mûr	Mature
Mûrir	Mature
Muscat	Muscat

French	English
Muscaté	Muscat Like
Muselage	Mucilage
Muselet	Muselet/Wire Cage (For Champagne Corks)
Muselet	Wire Cage/Muselet (For Champagne Corks)
Neutre	Neutral
Nez	Nose
Nez Oxydé	Maderized (Oxidized Aroma)
Nez Oxydé	Oxidized Nose/ Maderized
Noix	Walnut
Noix De Muscade	Nutmeg
Note	Hint
Notes D'évolution	Development Notes
Notes De Bois	Oak Hints
Notes Minérales	Mineraly
Nouveau	New
Nuances	Hues
Nuances	Nuances

French	English
Odeur D'ail	Garlicy
Œnologie	Winemaking/Enology
Œnologie	Enology/Winemaking
Œnologue	Winemaker/Enologist
Œnologue	Enologist/Winemaker
Œnophile	Enophile
Œufs Pourris	Rotten Egg
Olfactif	Smelling Phase
Onctueux	Unctuous (Overly Sweet)
Opalescent	Opalescent
Opaque	Opaque
Organoleptique	Organoleptic
Outre	Wineskin/Bota Bag
Ouvert	Open
Oxydation	Oxidation
Oxydé	Oxidized
Paillé	Straw (Color)
Pâle	Pale
Pamplemousse	Grapefruit

French	English
Panier-Verseur	Decanting Basket/ Cradle
Panier-Verseur	Decanting Cradle/ Basket
Parfumé	Perfumed
Particules Solides En Suspension	Suspended Solids
Passerillage	Raising
Pasteurisation	Pasteurization
Pasteuriser	Pasteurize
Pâteux	Paste Like
Pâtisserie	Bakery
Pauvre	Impoverished
Pellicule	Skin
Pellicule Mûre	Ripe Skin
Pénétrant	Overwhelming/ Penetrating (Aroma Or Taste)
Pénétrant	Penetrating/ Overwhelming (Aroma Or Taste)
Pépin	Grape Seed
Pépin	Seed

French	English
Perce	Tap (To Tap Barrel)
Persistance	Persistence
Petit Vin/Maigre	Meager (Lacking Flavor)
Phénol	Phenol
Phénolique	Phenolic
Piquant	Spicy Hot
Pointe	Hot (Alcohol)
Poivron	Bell Pepper
Polyphénol	Polyphenol
Pomme Verte	Green Apples
Pompage	Pumping
Potentialité	Potentiality
Pourpre	Purple
Pourriture Noble	Botrytis Cinerea (Noble Rot)
Pourriture Noble	Noble Rot (Botrytis Cinerea)
Précipitation	Precipitation
Précipiter	Precipitate
Premium	Premium

French	English
Presser	Press (To)
Pressoir	Wine Press
Pressoir	Wine Press
Pressurage	Pressing
Producteur	Grower
Producteur	Producer
Productif	Productive
Productivité	Productivity
Propre	Clear
Pruine	Bloom
Prune	Plum
Pulpe	Pulp
Pupitre	Shaking Table
Pureté	Purity
Rafle	Stalk
Rafle	Stalk
Rafraîchir	Refresh
Raisin	Grape
Raisin De Table	Table Grape
Rappeler	Recall

French	English
Récolte	Harvest (To)
Réduction	Reduction
Réfractomètre	Refractometer
Réfractométrie	Refractometry
Remontage	Riddling
Remonter	Pump Over
Remuage/Brassage	Stirring Up
Rendement	Yield
Renfermé/Fermé	Closed
Repos	Rest
Reposer	Rest
Réserve	Reserve
Résine	Resin
Respiration	Breathing
Robinet	Tap (On A Barrel)
Robuste	Robust
Rond	Round
Rondeur	Roundness
Rosé	Rosé
Rouge	Red

French	English
Rouge	Red (For Wine)
Rouge Cerise	Cherry Red (Color)
Rouge Feu	Fire Engine Red
Rouge Jaunâtre	Yellowish Red/Bricky
Rouge Jaunâtre	Bricky/Yellowish Red
Rouleau	Roller
Roussi	Singed
Rubis	Ruby
Sabler	Polish (Sandblast)
Satiné	Shiny
Saveur	Flavor
Saveur De Madère	Sherrified/Maderized
Saveur Du Sherry	Sherrified/Maderized
Saveur En Bouche	Mouthfeel
Saveur/Goût	Palate
Savoureux	Flavorful
Scintillement	Highlights
Sec/Sèche	Dry
Seconde Fermentation	Secondary Fermentation
Sédiment/Dépôt	Sediment

French	English
Sérieux	Serious
Sirop	Syrup
Sommelier	Wine Steward
Somptueux	Sumptuous
Soufre	Sulphur
Soufré (Vin)	Sulfurous
Soutirer	Rack
Soyeux	Silky
Stabilisation	Stabilisation
Stabiliser	Stabilise
Stable	Stable
Stockage	Storage
Structure	Structure
Suave	Soft
Subtil	Subtle
Sucre Résiduel	Residual Sugar
Sulfate	Sulfate
Sulfitage	Sulfited
Taché	Stained
Tanin	Tannin

French	English
Tanique	Tannic
Tardif	Late
Tartrate	Tartrate
Teinte	Hue
Teintes	Highlights
Température Ambiante	Room Temperature
Ténacité	Tenacity
Tendre	Tenderness
Terpène	Terpene
Terpénique	Terpenic
Terreux	Earthy
Terroir	Terroir
Texture	Texture
Tirage/Soutirage	Racking
Tonalité	Hue
Tonalité	Hue
Tonnelier	Cooper
Tonnellerie	Cooperage
Touche	Feel
Transport	Transport

French	English
Transporter	Transport (To)
Trou	Hollow
Trouble	Turbid
Truffe	Truffle
Tube	Wine Pipe
Turbidité	Turbidity
Tuyau	Hose
Vanille	Vanilla
Vanillé	Vanilla
Velouté	Velvety
Vendange	Harvest (The)
Vendange Tardive	Late Harvest
Verdeur	Greenness/Herbaceous
Verdeur	Herbaceous/Greenness
Verju	Green Wine
Vernis	Varnish
Vert	Green
Vieillir	Age
Vieillissement	Aged

French	English
Vieillissement	Aging
Vieillissement/Élevage	Aged
Vigne	Grapevine
Vignoble	Vineyard
Vigoureux	Vigorous
Vin	Wine
Vin Alcoolisé	Fortified Wine
Vin De Base	Base Wine
Vin De Cépage	Varietal
Vin De Cépage	Varietal Wine
Vin De Garde	Aged Wine
Vin De Goutte	First Press Wine
Vin De L'année	New (Nouveau) Wine
Vin De Liqueur	Fortified Wine
Vin De Paille	Raisin Wine
Vin De Paille	Straw Wine
Vin De Presse	Press Wine
Vin De Table	Table Wine
Vin Doux	Dessert/Sweet Wine
Vin Doux	Sweet/Dessert Wine

French	English
Vin Emblématique	Icon Wine
Vin En Carafe/En Pichet	Wine In Carafe
Vin En Vrac	Bulk Wine
Vin Fortifié	Fortified Wine
Vin Généreux	Big/Generous Wine
Vin Généreux	Generous/Big Wine
Vin Mousseux	Sparkling Wine
Vin Ordinaire	Ordinary Wine
Vin Pétillant	Slightly Sparkling Wine
Vin Tranquille	Still Wine
Vinification	Vinification/Wine-Making
Vinosité	Vinous
Violacé	Violet (Color)
Viscosité	Viscosity
Visqueux	Viscous
Visuel	Visual Phase
Viticulture	Viticulture
Vitiviniculture	Winemaking And Grape Growing

French	English
Vivace	Crisp
Voluptueux	Voluptuous
Zeste D'orange	Orange Peel
Zimuría	Zymurgy

Suggestions? Corrections?

Info@BandCPublishing.Com